Jungle/Drum 'n'
for the acoustic dr

A GUIDE TO APPLYING TODAY'S ELECTRONIC MUSIC TO THE DRUM SET

by Johnny Rabb

Jungle/Drum 'n' Bass
for the acoustic drum set
A GUIDE TO APPLYING TODAY'S ELECTRONIC MUSIC TO THE DRUM SET

by Johnny Rabb

■

Project Manager
Ray Brych

■

Cover Photo
Rick Malkin

■

Photography
Rick Malkin, Ed Sargent, Gregg Lohman

■

Cover Design
Jim Stelluto, Mike Duncan, Ed Uribe

■

Design and Layout
Dancing Planet® MediaWorks™

■

Music Typesetting
Gregg Lohman and Ed Uribe

■

Audio Recording and Mixing
Jim Stelluto and Shane Gue at Entropy Recording, Nashville, TN

■

Audio Mastering
Ed Uribe at Dancing Planet® MediaWorks™, Cresskill, NJ

■

All music composed and performed by
Johnny Rabb

■

Music Transcriptions of Johnny Rabb's Grooves
Gregg Lohman

■

Additional Editing
Ed Uribe, Gregg Lohman, Ray Brych

Foreword

By Steve Smith

U.S. drumming evolved through innovative players reflecting the sounds and rhythms of the culture while influencing those sounds and rhythms with their own unique concepts. Johnny Rabb is such a drummer—he embodies and expands upon the percussive voice of today's youth culture. His approach to jungle/drum 'n' bass for the acoustic drum set is revolutionary in a world of acoustic/electric drumset hybrids and computer-programmed samples. He plays the jungle/drum 'n' bass grooves on an acoustic drum set, producing astonishingly electronic-like sounds—organically. In this book he shares his concepts and discoveries with us.

I've seen Johnny Rabb in clinic and was impressed with his beautiful touch on the instrument—he doesn't "slam" the drums but plays them with finesse, extracting a full sound and grooving with an exciting yet relaxed feel. He enhances his encyclopedic vocabulary and knowledge of jungle/drum 'n' bass drumming with his unique use of cymbals on drums and his own invention, the johnnyraBB RhythmSaw Drumsticks. For me, the *coup de gras* was his extraordinary control with the Freehand Technique. I had always considered that technique merely an interesting drum trick until Johnny demonstrated that the Freehand Technique can also be a very usable and musical technique—in the correct hands.

Recently I've developed an interest in the jungle/drum 'n' bass grooves because they are new, exciting, fast, hard-to-play, and sound great! On my Vital Information recording *Show 'Em Where You Live*, I played a tune called "The Fire Still Burns" using the jungle/drum 'n' bass approach. I, too, use an acoustic drum set, but I hadn't thought of incorporating any electronic-like sounds into my set at the time of the recording. Not long ago Johnny and I jammed at a drum clinic and I realized that I'm just scratching the surface of this new drumming concept. I'm inspired by Johnny's book and intend on spending more time with it, adding some new ideas to my repertoire!

For those of you already playing jungle/drum 'n' bass grooves, this book will definitely open up some great new ideas to you. If you've never tried playing jungle/drum 'n' bass grooves, let this book introduce you to something new. Listen to the music, open your mind, and get to work on Johnny Rabb's *Jungle/Drum 'n' Bass for the Acoustic Drum Set*.

Steve Smith

June 2001

Hanging out with Steve Smith after an intense jungle jam at PPC Music's Drum Night 2001 in Hanover, Germany

Acknowledgments

Thanks to my family and friends: My mom and dad, Charlie and Norma Rabb, for their love and lifelong support of my career. Thanks to my amazing wife Jacqui for her love, friendship, and advice; Gregg Lohman for his friendship and extra time involved in this project; Ed Sargent; Steve Smith for being such a major inspiration and being involved with this project; Ray Brych; Ed Uribe; Mike and Jared Rabb; Michael Lawson; Ryano; John Aldridge; Jim Keltner; Rikki Rockett; Zoro; Matt Savage (aka Haddock); Steven and Simone Byrom; Robin Tolleson; Fred Coury; Craig Faniani; Kathie Williams; Boo McAffee; Craig Alan; Matt, Melinda, and Macy Curtis; Nick and Rose Willow; Scott Reams; the Garlan family; Greg Moutafis; Kerrie and Dustin Youngdahl; Marco Minnemann; Thomas Lang; MikeSnyder; Rick Malkin; Jim Stelluto; Shane Gue; Colleen Curtis; John McTigue III; Chris Patterson; Jerry Navarro; Frank Jearson; Floyd Downing; G.W. Pope; Harry McCarthy and family at Drum Paradise; Steve Fisher; John Aldridge; Bryan and Traci Frasher; Larry Tagg; Bob Williams; Jeff Jetton; Jay Weaver; Jeff and Kim Marino; Berklee College of Music Percussion and Music Education staff; Steve "Dub" Wilkes and Ginny; Johan Svensson; Marko Djordjevic; Takeshi Ichikawa; Ed Kaspik; John Ramsey; Bob Tamagni; Skip Hadden; John Hazilla; Ian Froman; Joel Rosenblatt; Clyde Stubblefield; John "Jabo" Starks; and Six Drumsets. Special thanks for the musical inspiration from all of you I have had the opportunity to meet at performances, clinics, or trade shows throughout my career.

MEINL Cymbals and Percussion: Norbert Saemann, Udo Heubeck, Reinhold Meinl, Richard Boveri, and the entire MEINL company. **Pro-Mark Drumsicks:** Pat Brown, Maury Brochstein, Kevin Radomski. **REMO Drumheads:** Matt Connors, Michelle Jacoby, Chris Hart, and all at Remo. **Drum Workshop:** Don Lombardi, John Good, Chris Lombardi, Juels Thomas. Garrison, Scott Donnell, and Dave Levine. **DrumFrame:** Bob Gatzen. **AUDIX Microphones:** Rob Schnell and Cliff Castle. **DRUMOMETER:** Boo McAfee and Craig Alan. **Grip Peddler:** Steven Adams. **MadWaves:** Laurie Rich and all at MadWaves. **C-Shirtz:** Chuck Hester.

 DRUMOMETER

A very special thanks to Gregg Lohman for being a true friend and for his time spent on notation, transcription, typing, and editing. His eyes and ears were a big help in making this project a reality.

Gregg Lohman is a freelance drummer/percussionist in the Nashville area and currently plays with country artist Aaron Tippin as well as with his original band, Raisin' Cain. He received a master's degree in music performance from the University of Tennessee–Knoxville and a bachelor's degree in music performance from Eastern Illinois University.

Special thanks to: Ray Brych, Gregg Lohman, and Ed Uribe for seeing this project through from inception to layout and finally the finished product. I couldn't have done it without you.

Warner Bros. Publications: Thank you to all the staff at Warner Bros. Publications. This book would not have been possible without the support and work from the following people: Ray Brych, David Hakim, Mike Finkelstein, Jason Beals, Karl Bork, Larry Kornblum, and Ken Hagen.

Me with the Warner Bros. gang. L-R: Dave Hakim, me, Mike Finkelstein, and Ray Brych

About the Author

Johnny Rabb received his first drum set at the tender age of three. With the support of his parents and the influence of live concerts and instructional clinics, Johnny began to excel at a tremendous rate. Johnny's dedication to his new love and eventual life's pursuit led him to the prestigious Berklee College of Music to pursue degrees in education and performance.

After the course of study and musical experimentation, Johnny relocated to Nashville, Tennessee, where he invented the award-winning RhythmSaw and shared in the design and manufacturing of drumsticks and percussion accessories under the company name johnnyraBB Drumsticks. Johnny has now moved on to endorse Pro-Mark drumsticks, where he has developed his own signature line.

Johnny's move to Nashville proved to be the launchpad needed for the development of a dream studio. Playing with touring notables such as Tanya Tucker, Hank Williams III, and Maynard Ferguson provided the excitement of live performances along with the creative contribution of writing and developing educational books/videos and workshops.

Johnny was asked to participate in an event sponsored by the Nashville Percussion Institute by founder Boo McAfee. Johnny has the uncanny ability to play single-stroke rolls at an incredible speed. With the assistance of McAfee and a device named the DRUMOMETER, the first competition for The World's Fastest Drummer was born. Johnny won hands down and in doing so came to the attention of the Guinness World Records committee. Johnny was asked to defend his title live at the Guinness World Records Experience in Orlando, Florida. The attempt was documented by VH-1 for a show called "Rock & Roll Record Breakers." Johnny not only defended but also broke the existing world record of 1,026 by playing 1,071 single strokes in 60 seconds. The opportunity to be a part of such an elite group via his chosen instrument in life is truly a great honor. Johnny is featured in several interactive displays at the Guinness World Attractions including those in Orlando, Florida; Gatlinburg, Tennessee; Hollywood, California; and Copenhagen, Denmark.

Johnny is currently participating in numerous clinics throughout the world to outstanding reviews. He performed a memorable show to a capacity crowd at the Montreal Drumfest and also performed in France, in Italy, and at the Musikmesse in Frankfurt, Germany. Johnny continues to perform clinics on both acoustic and electric drums. He currently is a product demonstrator for the Roland Corp. He was honored to play at the Percussive Arts Society International Convention in Nashville, Tennessee.

Johnny continues to develop and contribute to both the industry and the community. He has published his own instructional drum videos, children's books, and solo album. He has also designed "The Rabb Pack," a signature series of cymbals for the MEINL Cymbal Company. Johnny believes that education is the most important element for the future and continues to find opportunities to share his knowledge with musicians worldwide.

Johnny has recently completed the MEINL Generation X Days European tour with Thomas Lang and Marco Minnemann, and the ROLAND/DW Sound Lab Tour with drum artist Mike Snyder.

Germany 2001

Backstage at Musikmesse, Frankfurt

Masterclass at Musikmesse

*Me and Roland Peil performing
at Musikmesse*

PPC Music's Drum Night

Table of Contents

Note: The two audio example CDs accompanying this book are designed to enhance your learning experience.
Audio example CD 1: Consists of tuning examples, book exercises, and advanced sound exercises from the individual chapters. You can use CD 1 in direct reference to the text.
Audio example CD 2: Consists of basic electronics, hybrid drum setups, breaking the rules, one track from Johnny's solo album *Acoustic Machine*, and groove loops.
Groove Loops: Original jungle/drum 'n' bass play-along tracks for you to practice any exercise from the book.

Chapter 4: Basic Rolls and Buzzes · 55

Chapter 5: Unison Jungle · 69

Chapter 6: Linear Jungle Grooves · 89

Chapter 7: Hi-Hat Exercises · 103

Chapter 8: Multiple Snare Jungle Grooves · 107

Chapter 16: Putting It All Together _____ **149**

Appendix _____ **151**

Performing at Frankfurt Musikmesse 2001

Introduction

This book should be used as a guide on how to play jungle/drum 'n' bass on the acoustic drum set. No matter what background you have, I am hoping that you will be able to pick up a pair of sticks, get behind the kit, and begin to play as soon as you look at the first exercise. This is not intended to be a history book. However, I am very interested in the history of this style of music and research it any chance I get. I am constantly learning new things about jungle and drum 'n' bass music. My mission is to show you how to establish a solid foundation in this style.

The exercises provided are based on my approach to playing these styles of grooves on the drum set. My goal is that when you listen to the music, you will be able to relate to the material in this book. You will learn new techniques on how to make the music sound electronic with little or no electronics at all. You will primarily be using the bass drum, snare drum, and hi-hat/ride cymbal as your main sources and can practice the majority of the book with this basic setup. As the book progresses, we will be adding different instruments and accessories to the drum set, simulating what is heard on the recordings from today's jungle/drum 'n' bass artists and DJs.

People like Ed Uribe and Robbie Ameen among many others have written Latin books that utilize the Cuban rhythm sections—congas, timbales, bongos, bell, and so on. For example, there are exercises using the cowbell with the right hand, conga pattern on the rack tom, clave with the left foot, and so forth. I use a similar approach, taking the many parts of a drum machine or sampler and applying them to the drum set. Since there are so many sounds layered, looped, and sampled in jungle/drum 'n' bass, my main objective was to simulate the electronics on the acoustic drum set.

What Is Jungle/Drum 'n' Bass?

To me jungle/drum 'n' bass is a high-energy, fast-paced new trend of music that is popping up everywhere. You hear it frequently on TV, on a lot of underground/college radio stations, and at many clubs. Since this music is so energetic, it is used in many TV commercials and on movie soundtracks. To me jungle/drum 'n' bass is comprised of several basic groove variations. It is almost like a dictionary of terms that make up each groove. The music is more instrumental, hence the term *drum 'n' bass*. It is literally drums and bass—drum set or electronic drums with sub bass and low tones underneath, generally ranging from 140 to 180 beats per minute. Most pieces of music are accompanied by strong synthesizer or string lines as melodies. Even though the music is mostly instrumental, there are many groups and projects that do use lyrics and vocals. Artists from pop to jazz have adopted these quick and catchy grooves and have applied them to their own style.

Jungle/Drum 'n' Bass is the title I came up for my book. Even though these styles are similar, they do have their differences. The difference between jungle and drum 'n' bass is fairly simple. Jungle is more random and syncopated using sixteenth notes within the groove. Drum 'n' bass grooves are much simpler grooves and usually slightly slower in tempo. When you get more involved in this style of music, you will realize there are many styles under the category jungle or drum 'n' bass, such as jump up, hard step, and so on. The exercises in this book should give you a solid foundation covering both jungle and drum 'n' bass styles.

Where Can You Find It?

You can find jungle/drum 'n' bass music almost everywhere you turn. Some people have no idea they are hearing it. It is on TV commercials (Sony, Nike, Volkswagen, Timex, Quaker Oatmeal). It is fast-paced music that gets the product to seem more sporty and energetic. I have heard jungle and drum 'n' bass music used for commercials, cartoons, movies, and other soundtracks. Everyone is catching on to the fad and realizing how cool and infectious it is.

There are many groups that perform jungle and drum 'n' bass live. A few of them are Soul Coughing, Jungle Funk, and LAKETROUT. Medeski, Martin, and Wood simulate dance/techno music in a jazz sense live, and they are incredible. Even David Bowie added some jungle grooves on one of his past albums. One of my favorite recordings is from the Fiona Apple hit "Fast as You Can," played by Matt Chamberlain. He lays down a totally original groove that makes the song come alive. Start to listen to all types of music and see if you can pick up on people and places using these grooves because it is definitely worth checking out.

How I Got Started

Approximately seven years ago, a friend of mine asked me if I had ever heard of jungle music. Although it was already popular among the underground, I had not yet been exposed. My first listening experience came from a compilation album called *Jungle Vibes* featuring various artists. The first time I heard it, I became obsessed with the music and immediately started to imitate it on the drum set. I listened, transcribed, played along to it, and became addicted to the way it grooved and how it felt. It was mainly all programmed using drum machines, sampling CDs, and loops. At that moment I realized I wanted to write a book about jungle/drum 'n' bass drumming. I began compiling transcriptions of the music, playing along to records, and introducing jungle/drum 'n' bass music when I was doing my acid jazz, hip-hop gigs with my old group, Stickboy, in Sacramento, California.

DJ Goldie, who was the first DJ I heard of at the time, was my first purchase. From there I bought and checked out anything I could that had to do with jungle/drum 'n' bass. The next thing I started noticing was that the music started popping up on TV jingles/commercials. I also realized when I toured Belgium that jungle/drum 'n' bass was really hitting overseas. I knew I was way out of touch from places like New York and abroad. I was playing hip-hop and acid jazz at my gigs back home. At that time, acid jazz was very popular in the San Francisco bay area—acid jazz being more half-time-oriented grooves or funky old-school loops with DJs and horns. Some of the acid jazz records in my collection were hinting at jungle by throwing double-time over the top of the half-time grooves. At the time I didn't realize this was a style. I just thought it was interesting and original drum machine programming!

I played at the NAMM show in Los Angeles demonstrating my take on jungle/drum 'n' bass. That is where I met Tony Verderosa, who is not only a monster drummer but also a one-man band. His approach to this style is amazing. At the same show I met Zach Danziger, who is another fantastic drummer. As I became more immersed in this style, I began to meet other drummers who love jungle/drum 'n' bass. Jojo Mayer and Yuval Gabay (Soul Coughing) are two other drummers I have met who are totally into this scene. It is always fun to see these guys and hear their take on this style.

My hope is that in the future we will see a lot more guys and girls playing this style live. The most fascinating thing to me is that every player I meet has his or her own personal techniques that he or she uses to simulate jungle/drum 'n' bass grooves on the acoustic drum set. I have been studying and learning about this style for the past seven years. Although I have a genuine passion for most music genres, I find myself infatuated with jungle/drum 'n' bass music.

Samplers

The use of samplers is very important when writing/recording jungle and drum 'n' bass music. A sampler is basically a digital recorder. It records sounds or beats that can be edited or looped. Looping a beat simply means recording a drum groove into the sampler and having it repeat over and over. The loop is edited to ensure it is the correct length so it can repeat or loop in time. A beat can also be cut into fragments, which are sometimes as short as one beat or as long as multiple measures. This will allow the composer to have multiple drum-set sounds in the same bar. (Check out Basic Electronics, DISC 2, TR 1, for an audio example of the BOSS SP-303 phrase sampler in action).

Many composers choose to use computers (Mac or PC) to exercise their songwriting skills. Programs like Acid are extremely user-friendly. There is also a new program called Reason that really allows almost anyone to make a futuristic record! As soon as you download your sounds into the computer, you can start creating your own music with a click of the mouse. There is some learning that has to take place before you can actually compose a complete album, but most of these programs are relatively simple to get the hang of. I believe that technology is a great creative-writing tool when used in a musical way. Today's music is advanced and does not require going into a recording studio all of the time. In my case, I use a sequencer like the Roland MC-505 and my SP-303 Phrase Sampler for the majority of my writing. They are very simple to use and have great internal sounds. These days computers seem to be the norm. If you don't have a computer, you should definitely get one. Finally, If you play drums, expand your musicianship and learn how to play keyboards (piano), and start writing! There is no reason not to express your musicianship to its fullest.

Sampling CDs

Sampling CDs are a major element in producing and writing jungle and drum 'n' bass music. There are companies such as Sonic Foundry and East West, to name a couple, that produce and distribute these CDs. Sampling CDs come in two versions, audio or CD-ROM. The audio format allows you to play the CD like you would any other album you own. Then you can sample a measure and then loop it or chop it up. The CD-ROM version is formatted to work for specific samplers. You then can buy the CD-ROM for your specific brand of sampler, for example, AKAI, Digidesign, E-MU, Ensoniq, and Kurzweil. The samples are then taken and used for songs.

Since a sampler can hold multiple samples, the drum-set sounds can be totally different. In some songs it is normal to hear a variety of different drum set sounds. These CDs range in prices anywhere from $30 for a single audio sampling CD to $500 or more for a complete CD library. The CD-ROM format is generally more expensive since it is formatted especially for a specific brand of sampler. There are a ton of license-free sampling CDs available. The term *license-free* simply means that by purchasing the CD, the owner has the right to use any sound or groove from the CD in an original piece of music without paying any royalties or licensing fees. Generally the distributor will give the artist a royalty for each CD sold.

I recorded an acid jazz sampling CD with my friend Scott Reams, a great engineer, singer, songwriter, and producer. For this sampling CD, we used many different drum sets and had about ten hours of tape. I am in the process of completing my own library of drum sounds and loops ranging from jungle to house and acid jazz. I would be very excited to have people use my original grooves on their projects. I look at it as a way to drum on other people's songs without physically being there!

The first audio sampling CD I purchased was *Jungle Warfare III*. This CD consists of numerous programmed jungle drum breaks. I transcribed the first few tracks of the CD to really understand what the programmer was doing. I then realized that there was a vocabulary of fragments and phrases. The fragments consisted of sixteenth, eighth, and quarter notes mixed together. When referring to the records I previously listened to, I realized that most of the DJs were using the grooves from the *Jungle Warfare III* album.

Contributing to the Future
An Interview with Clyde Stubblefield

We all know Clyde Stubblefield, John "Jabo" Starks, and Bernard Purdie as the original funk drummers. They are just a few of the many drummers who pioneered the way funk sounded and was played. A lot of the grooves found in today's jungle and drum 'n' bass music have been influenced by original grooves from the likes of these great players. In one specific example, I heard a James Brown groove sped up. This example can be found on the opening theme for "The Powerpuff Girls," which airs on the Cartoon Network. If you listen closely, you can hear that the groove is taken from "The Funky Drummer Re-Mix" (from the James Brown album *In the Jungle Groove*), on which Clyde Stubblefield performed. The exact groove was sampled and then sped up to approximately 160 bpm. I had the pleasure of talking to Clyde about this issue, and below are some of his own words.

Johnny: Do you realize that your groove from "The Funky Drummer Re-Mix" is used in the theme song for "The Powerpuff Girls" only at a faster tempo?

Clyde Stubblefield: You heard the cartoon playing this pattern and you knew it was me. That is some of the stuff that has been happening. They change the tempo on it and make it sound like something else. I am very happy and proud of people using my drum patterns. Other people like you know that it is me even when I don't even realize that it is me. I have also put out a sampling CD with DNA and it is possible that they used a track off of that for the cartoon. I made my sampling CD for the purpose of being used by people other than myself.

J. R.: In the past, people have taken your grooves without giving credit or without paying royalties and used them all over the place for hip-hop, rap, and other forms of music. Since you have recorded your own sampling CD, do you feel like you have gained back what was taken from you without your consent?

C. S.: No, not at all. This is just a little drop in the bucket for my sampling CDs. I couldn't credit anything in the past because I did not own it. Even though they were my original drum patterns, I was never compensated for past grooves. My sampling CD has not even come close to what I feel I deserve from my grooves being used on other people's songs. If I could have gotten the press, credit, or acknowledgment from the artists that used my grooves, I would be happy. It means a lot more than money. If I was an important element to the music, please acknowledge me. Don't use my stuff and make millions off of it and look over me. I don't look at the money aspect, I just feel that it is very disrespectful to use my beats to make a song and not acknowledge my work.

J. R.: Did you ever think that "The Funky Drummer" would be used for all of these styles including jungle and drum 'n' bass? That beat sounds fantastic at any tempo.

C. S: To me, I never thought any of our patterns or drumbeats would amount to anything. I just thought I was just laying down beats for James Brown. I never made a pattern to be used as a sample back then. It was just what I came up with at the time. I tell everybody [laughing] I don't even like "The Funky Drummer" that much because it was just something that I thought of at that moment that didn't even strike me, and it didn't have anything I wanted, but it worked. Everyone else seemed to like it and I didn't understand it. I cannot understand why they chose that particular beat to sample so much! [chuckling] You know, there's a lot of other stuff!

J. R.: How does it make you feel to know that you have contributed to jungle and drum 'n' bass without even realizing it?

C.S: Right now if I turned on that cartoon, I might hear "Funky" ["The Funky Drummer Groove"], but I am still not sure that it is me. I would love for something like that to be me, but I still have a hard time putting me in that picture. I think, man, that is a hot drum pattern; however, I don't sit and think that it's me. If I could get anything out of this, I would really appreciate getting the credit for my work. They use all of our stuff—me and "Jabo" Starks— and they aren't giving us any kind of thank-you or anything.

Before the end of the interview, I told Clyde I believe it is definitely his groove at a faster tempo on "The Powerpuff Girls" theme song! I want to thank Clyde for being such an inspiration to my playing and a true gentleman. His original playing style has influenced music in the past and the present, and it continues into the future.

L-R: Ed Sargent, John "Jabo" Starks, Bernard Purdie, Clyde Stubblefield, and me at the NAMM Show in Los Angeles, CA, 2001

France 2001

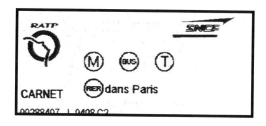

Performing at Percu-Tours

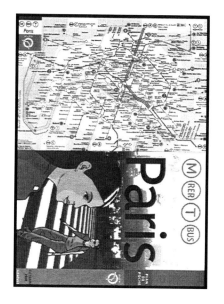

Setup and Sounds

Because jungle/drum 'n' bass grooves are extremely quick, I needed to figure out the right drum sounds to simulate this high-energy electronic music. The drums sounded higher in pitch because the samples were sped up. I started to concentrate on how to obtain electronic sounds from my acoustic drum set. I decided to use three snare drums in my setup to achieve the sounds I was hearing. I use a 14-inch snare drum for my main snare positioned directly in front of me. This gives me a nice thick backbeat and a great sound when I detune it to sound low and trashy. I use a 10-inch snare drum to the left of my hi-hat so I have the correct pitch when playing at faster tempos. The snare drums are an extremely important element in jungle/drum 'n' bass music. I feel that the three snare sizes used in my setup give me a colorful palette of sounds and a broad range of tuning options.

Often I will work on grooves using a small two-piece drum set (kick and snare) so I can focus on the speed and energy of the music. I have a 10-inch rack tom and 14-inch floor tom in my setup. I use these sparingly when approaching this style of drumming. I also have a single-headed 16-inch floor tom that I use as a hand bass drum. I use it to simulate the low tone of an 808 electronic bass drum. I have found that a 12-inch single-headed tom with a two-ply head also sounds amazing!

When I add electronics to my setup, I use the Roland SPD-20 and Hand-Sonic with the hi-hat trigger pedal and bass drum triggers. My different types of setups are as follows: a small acoustic kit, a large acoustic kit, a large acoustic/electronic hybrid kit, or all electronic. Each drum set is used for different situations depending on what sounds I want or need. In addition to the gear mentioned above, I also use the BOSS SP-303 phrase sampler and perform vocal percussion sounds using my AUDIX headset microphone.

You have probably noticed by now that I use the DrumFrame (shown in the three photos on this page) designed by innovative inventor/drummer Bob Gatzen. The comfort is amazing and allows my entire body the freedom to move about the drum set without discomfort or question. I have a hard time with my posture, and the DrumFrame gives me the opportunity to sit with correct posture, which aids my playing. Plus, it looks very cool and everything is exactly locked where I want it!

Drum Tuning Possibilities

E-ring placed on snare drum

When simulating jungle/drum 'n' bass grooves, your drumset will usually be tuned to sound very unorthodox.

Snare Drum

Try to detune your snare really low so it sounds like a low, processed, slow-speed, low-resolution sample. Another option is tuning the snare up to where it sounds high-pitched to simulate previous grooves that have been sped up. When using three snares, I like to use the 10-inch and 12-inch high-pitched and my main snare low-pitched so I can have the choice to go among the drums and have it sound like I am playing a different drum set. When appropriate for the style, I will place a T-shirt (old preferred!) over my snare drum to create a very muted snare sound. The Evans E-Ring is also a great way to mute the snare drum without completely choking it out. This works great when simulating this style.

T-shirt mute placed on snare drum

Bass Drum

I generally tune my bass drum three different ways. I use a wide open bass drum sound, dead bass drum sound, or an 18-inch bass drum with a jazz (open) tuning. I use a 20-inch bass drum the majority of the time. I use different head combinations to achieve the sound I am looking for. My all-around head of choice is the EVANS EMAD. This drumhead has an external muffling system that gives you the choice of a thin or thick foam ring for dampening. I almost always use one or two EQ pillows inside the bass drum to create a nice punchy sound with quick attack. In some instances I will leave it wide open without any dampening in the bass drum for a nice wide drum sound. The third way is to use my 18-inch DW bass drum and tune it like a jazz kick. This creates a whole new feel and more "boomy" sound.

8" and 10" Drumbals placed on snare drums

Hand Bass Drum

I use a 16-inch single-headed floor tom with an EVANS two-ply clear hydraulic drumhead. This drum allows me to have an open bass drum sound played with my left hand. Once again, a 12-inch tom works amazingly. Just try to find the right sound you are looking for.

Toms

Finally, I tune my toms in a fairly standard way using either EVANS G1 single-ply or G2 two-ply coated batter heads and G1 clears for the bottoms. The primary drums you will use are your snare drums and bass drum. Listen to some jungle and drum 'n' bass recordings and try to experiment with your own tuning ideas.

Cymbal Setup

The cymbals I have created with the Roland Meinl Company have enabled me to bring futuristic drumming to life. I needed to have a cymbal setup that allowed me the flexibility to play with a clean or trashy sound at any time. The combination of nickel-silver and brass cymbals gives me both sound options.

Tightening the wing nut to change the pitch of the Safari crash and ride cymbals

Safari Ride

With its unique sound waves, the 8-inch brass cymbal mounts on top of the 18-inch nickel-silver flat ride. The Safari crash and Safari ride cymbals give me a flat ride sound with a splash bell to simulate drum machine clap/trash effects. The Safari ride was designed with the Tension Tuning System, which allows you to tune the cymbal using the wing nut of the cymbal stand. (Check out the audio example on CD 1, Track 3).

Safari Crash

Safari Crash

The quick decay achieved by the two-cymbal combination is perfect for creating white noise, for simulating loops, for programmed grooves, or for effects. The 8-inch brass sound-wave splash cymbal mounts on top of the 16-inch nickel-silver flat crash. The Safari crash's decay and sound can also be manipulated using the Tension Tuning System.

Sound Wave Splash on Safari Hi-Hats

Safari Hi-Hats

The Safari hi-hats give me the raw sound I am looking for to re-create old breakbeats and loops. The bottom hat contains tambourine jingles, which enhance the sound spectrum. The combination of both top cymbals allows me to play in two different sound zones. These hi-hats provide a multitude of new sounds.

Safari Hi-Hats

Tension Tuning System (TTS)

Using the wing nut of the cymbal stand, you can tune the Safari ride and Safari crash to sound anywhere from trashy to virtually no decay. The Safari Hi-Hats can also be tuned to control the amount of trash by increasing or decreasing tension of the hi-hat clutch. The specially designed tension waves pressed into the cymbals enhance the trash effect. I can use all of the cymbals stacked or individually.

TTS (tension Tuning System) in action

Drumbals

Drumbals are cymbals that I designed to be placed and played on the drums. They are perfect for imitating white noise, hand-claps, and other electronic effects. I believe the Drumbals transform your drum set into an acoustic drum machine.

Practical Applications

By placing the Drumbal on the snare drum you can:

1. Hit the Drumbal with the stick, creating a clap similar to a drum machine.
2. Hit the snare drumhead, creating an electronic snare sound.
3. Use the snare head for ghost notes and the Drumbal for accents.

8" Drumbal

By holding the handle of the Drumbal you can:

1. Lift the Drumbal off the snare and slam it down, creating trashy accents.
2. (with snares off) Lift the Drumbal off and on the drumhead (with the hand) to change the pitch, similar to a talking drum.

Groove Tip: Drumbals can be moved to different drums, altering their pitch and sound. They will also fit directly in the drum (for example: a 10-inch Drumbal will fit perfectly in a 10-inch tom or snare), which will create the clap effect, or they can be placed on a larger drum, leaving room to play the remainder of the head. Drumbals are available from MEINL in two sizes: 8-inch and 10-inch.

Practice Tips

I recommend practicing with a drum machine like the Boss Dr. Rhythm DR-202 that has some dance-oriented music already preset as a practice tool. Another way is to practice to albums of all sorts or purchase a cheaper sampling CD and simulate it. If a sampling CD is way over budget, then grab a compilation at your nearest record store and use it as a play-along. It is very important to practice at various tempos. All of the examples in this book sound good slow as well as at faster tempos. If you have any ballads lying around the house, put them on and play double-time over the groove and turn them into jungle or drum 'n' bass tunes! Practicing away from the drum set is always a good idea. *Practice any groove from this book along with my seven original groove loops from audio CD 2.*

Practicing Away from the Drum Set

Try to check out different natural or mechanical sounds around you that can work for jungle/drum 'n' bass tempos. A basic idea is to listen for construction noises, city noise, a photocopier, anything! I use my turn signal in my car as a metronome and sing rhythms over it instead of singing to the radio. Anything that sounds percussive and rhythmic can easily be used as the basis for a groove. Please be careful if you do this in the car! Pay attention to what you are doing and drive safely.

Fragments Group A

Fragments provide a visual breakdown of rhythms used in each chapter. Some chapters contain a fragment group. Each individual fragment is a quarter note in length--one beat in 4/4 time. After you have practiced each fragment separately, you can choose any four fragments and combine them to create your own original one-bar grooves. Fragments will add to your originality and enhance your drumming vocabulary. *There are ten groups of fragments presented in this book: Groups A through J.*

Fragments Group A:

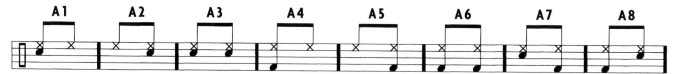

Fragment Groove Example:

Check out the example below. I simply chose four fragments and added them together. A7 + A4 + A1 + A5 = An original measure of groove! It is that simple.

Practice Tip: Once you have completed the book, you can go back and choose any fragment from any chapter and create endless groove and exercise ideas. To do this, simply choose any four fragments from any fragment grouping, grab some manuscript paper, and begin to create your new grooves! Remember, you cannot mess up. All you do is select four fragments at random, write them down on paper, and practice. It is also a great idea to create a binder of your fragment grooves. So, essentially you have two books in one! These grooves can be played as funk grooves, jungle grooves, or even swung hip-hop-style grooves. Don't be afraid to slow the metronome down and experiment with different styles and feels using the fragments.

Notation Key

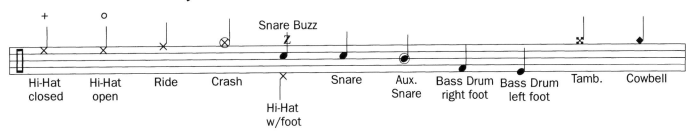

Hi-Hat closed | Hi-Hat open | Ride | Crash | Hi-Hat w/foot | Snare Buzz | Snare | Aux. Snare | Bass Drum right foot | Bass Drum left foot | Tamb. | Cowbell

Johnny's Drum Setup and Sounds

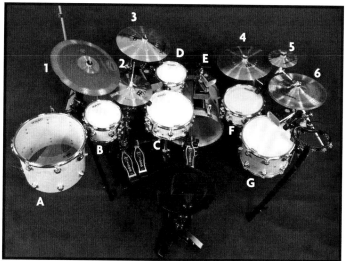

Cymbals and Percussion: Meinl
1. 18" One-of-a-Kind Thin Flat Ride w/Rivets (Champagne)
2. 14" Johnny Rabb Safari Hi-Hats
3. 16" Johnny Rabb Safari Crash
4. 18" Johnny Rabb Safari Ride
5. 10" Classic Splash (inverted – bottom); 10" Classic China Splash (top)
6. 16" Marathon Brass Mega Crash (bottom); 16" Classic China (top)

Realplayer Steelbells (STB80B-CH, STB80S-CH, STB625-CH, STB45-CH)
Tambourine (TMTB-BK)

Drums: Drum Workshop
A. 16" Hand Bass Drum
B. 5" x 10" Snare Drum
C. 5" x 14" Snare Drum
D. 8" x 10" Rack Tom
F. 5" x 12" Snare Drum
G. 12" x 14" Floor Tom
E. 16" x 20" Bass Drum

Drum Heads: Evans
Clear Hydraulic 2-ply (batter side only)
G1 Coated (top) – Snare Side (bottom)
G1 Orchestral (top) – Snare Side (bottom)
G1 Coated (top) – G1 Clear (bottom)
G1 Coated (top) – Snare Side (bottom)
G2 Coated (top) – G1 Clear (bottom)
EQ3 Batter or EMAD – Black Logo Head
with 2 Evans pillows

Hardware and Pedals: Drum Workshop on the DrumFrame
5 - Straight Boom Cymbal Stands with Short Boom (DW-CP-9700SB)
3 - Snare Stands (DW-CP-8300)
1 - Delta II Hi-Hat Stand (DW-CP-5500TD)
1 - Delta II Accelerator Double Pedal (DW-CP-5002AD)
1 - Tripod Throne (DW-CP-9100)
1 - $\frac{3}{8}$" Ball Joint
2 - Brackets for Cowbells

Microphones: Audix
Headset Microphone
Snare Drums-D1
Rack Tom-D3
Floor Tom-D4, Bass Drum D4XL
Overheads (2)-ADX-50

Drumsticks: Pro-Mark
Johnny Rabb Autograph Series

Electronics: Roland/MadWaves
SP-303 Phrase Sampler
HandSonic HPD-15 (see pg. 147)
SPD-20
MC-505
PMA-5
MadPlayer

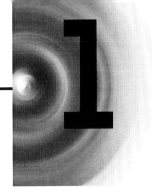

Preliminary Exercises

Gear needed for this chapter: kick, snare, hi-hat, and ride cymbal.
You can set up a drum kit with only these pieces to practice this section:

This section contains eighth-note and sixteenth-note Preliminary Exercises. These exercises will give you the basic foundation before moving forward in this book. Because jungle/drum 'n' bass music is played at such fast tempos, it is very important to practice these exercises to get your vocabulary together. Remember to START SLOWLY until you become proficient at each exercise. Then gradually increase the tempo once comfortable. Do not let the simplicity of the exercises fool you since the goal is to perform them smoothly at a quick tempo. The exercises may not sound quite like grooves, but these are some of the standard patterns that we will be using in upcoming chapters. Make sure you practice all of the following options:

Option 1: Top line hi-hat or ride/bottom line snare drum.

Option 2: Top line hi-hat or ride/bottom line bass drum.

Option 3: Top line hi-hat or ride/bottom line snare drum and bass drum (in unison).

Option 4: Top line hi-hat or ride/bottom line alternate between snare drum and bass drum (beginning with snare drum).

Option 5: Top line hi-hat or ride/bottom line alternate between bass drum and snare drum (beginning with bass drum).

Practice Tip: When practicing these exercises, remember to start slowly and to always use a metronome or drum machine. Listen to the audio example CD to make sure you are on the right track.

Eighth-Note Combinations

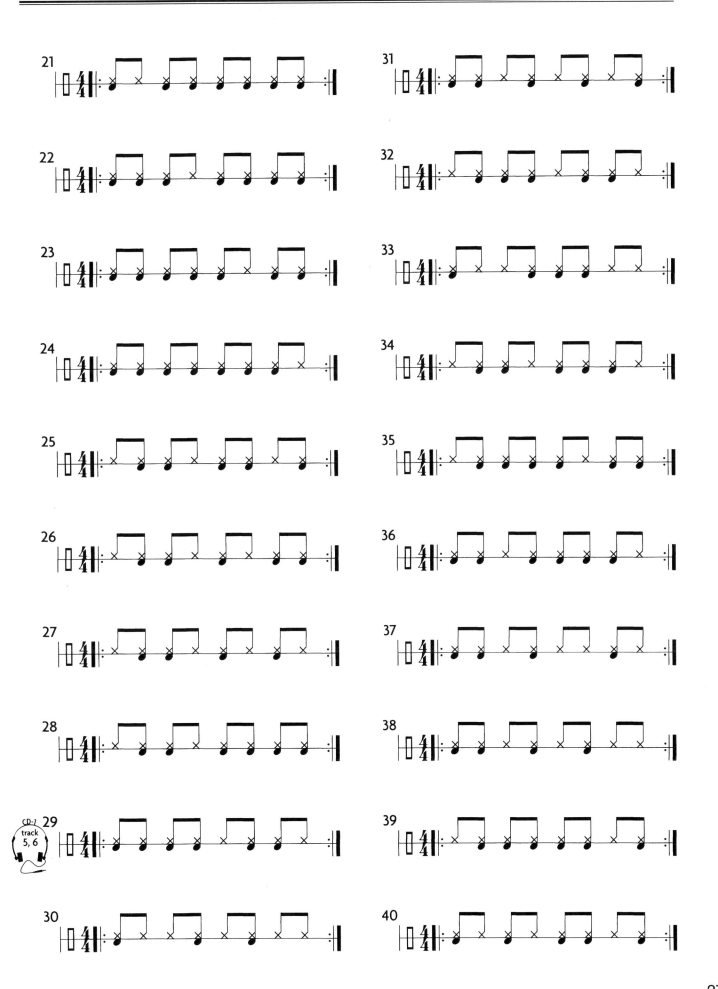

Eighth- and Sixteenth-Note Combinations

These exercises are designed to allow you to get familiar with note groupings that will appear throughout this book. It is important to subdivide and make sure that all sixteenth notes fall in the proper place when playing the exercises. Try to remember that we are simulating a programmed groove, so all notes should be short and staccato.

Examples: 3, 18, 32, 44

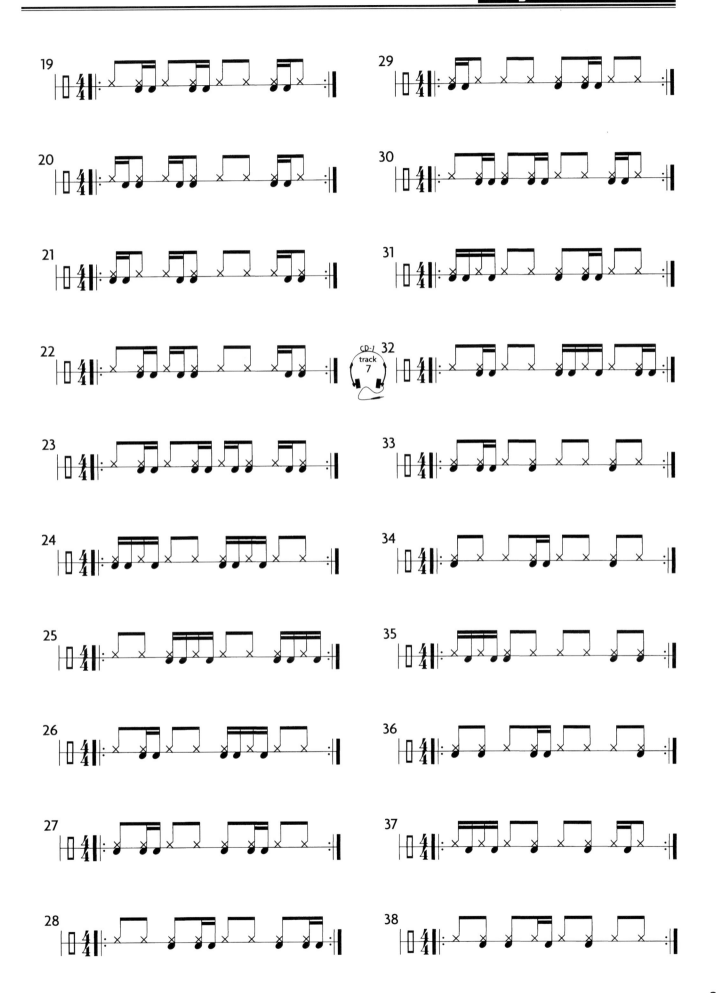

Eighth- and Sixteenth-Note Combinations (cont'd)

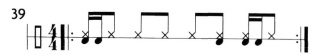

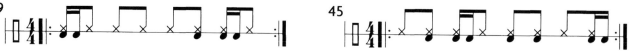

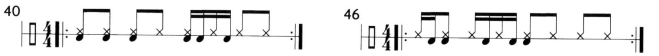

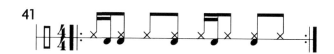

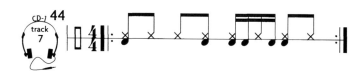

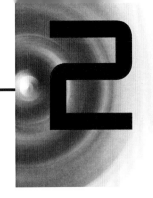

Eighth-Note Grooves

Gear needed for this chapter: kick, snare, hi-hat, and ride cymbal.
You can set up a drum kit with only these pieces to practice this section:

The purpose of this chapter is to get you comfortable with the basic feels in eighth-note format. It is important to practice the fragments by themselves before playing the exercises. Do not accentuate the downbeats or upbeats of the eighth notes on the hi-hat. They should all be played at equal dynamic levels. All of the snare drum and bass drum notes should be played at the same level in order to simulate the sound of the drum machine. It is important to become familiar with the sounds, patterns, and groupings of notes that are in today's jungle/drum 'n' bass grooves.

Listening Tip: Be sure to check out the audio example CD to get an idea of how to achieve the correct balance.

Fragments Group A: Eighth Notes

Eighth-Note Exercises: One Measure

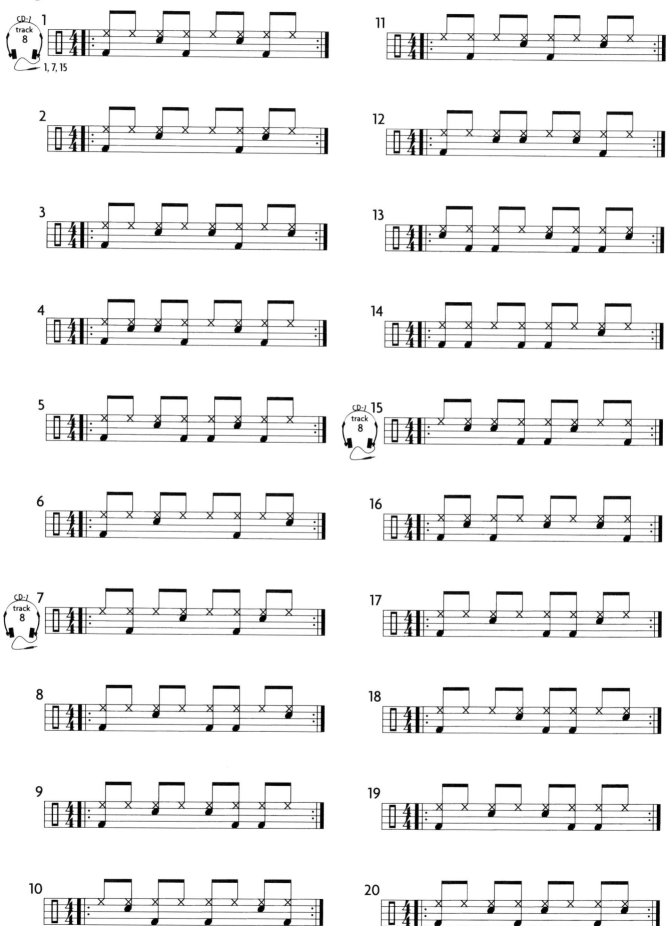

Eighth-Note Exercises: Two Measures

These exercises are designed to start getting your phrasing together. If needed, practice each measure individually and then when comfortable practice both measures together.

Examples: 1, 7, 13, 19, 27, 31, 37, 44, 49, 55

Eighth-Note Exercises: Two Measures (cont'd)

Eighth-Note Exercises: Two Measures (cont'd)

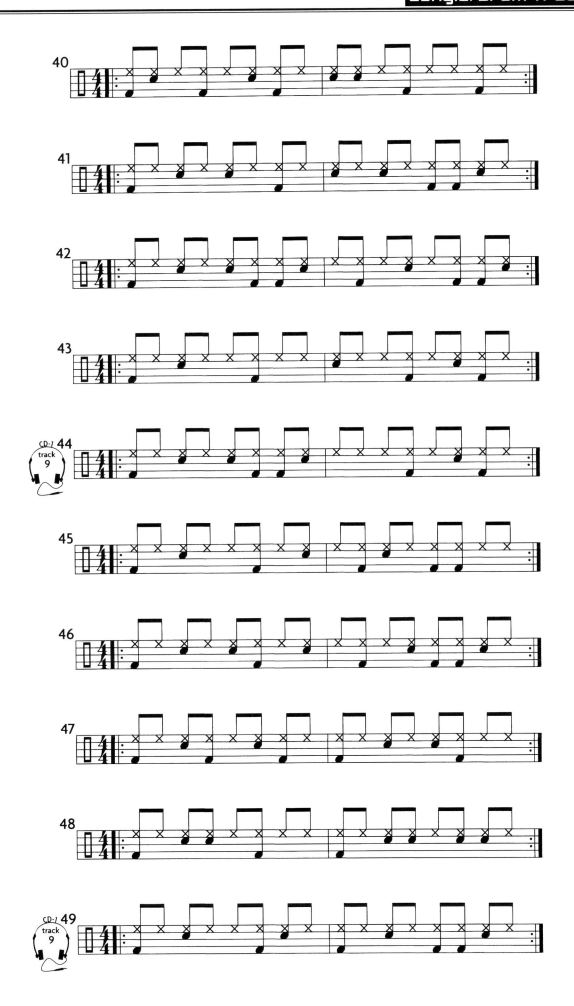

Eighth-Note Exercises: Two Measures (cont'd)

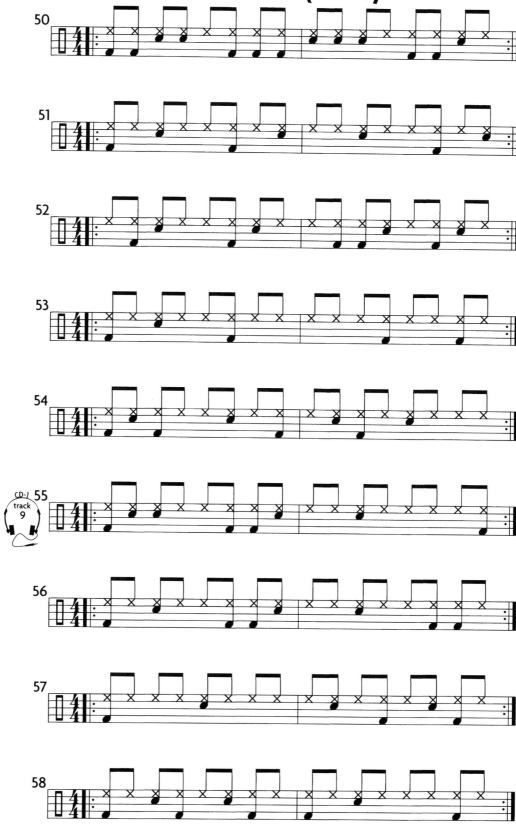

Eighth-Note Off-Beat Exercises: One Measure

These exercises can be tricky. If you are not familiar with this ostinato, take it SLOWLY! If needed, play the hi-hat and snare parts separately and then the same with hi-hat and bass drum. Finally, piece it all together into one groove.

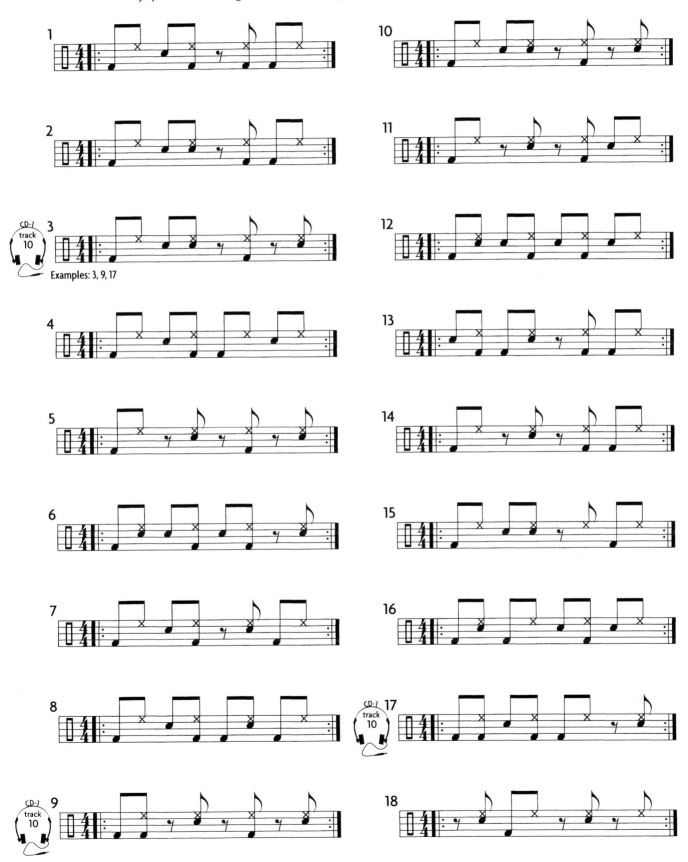

Examples: 3, 9, 17

Eighth-Note Off-Beat Exercises: One Measure (cont'd)

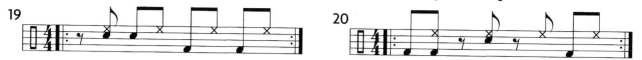

Eighth-Note Off-Beat Exercises: Two Measures

Examples: 1, 5, 9, 11, 17, 25, 27, 31

Eighth-Note Off-Beat Exercises: Two Measures (cont'd)

EVANS mainstage performance at DCI Buffalo, New York, 2001

Matt Savage and me at DCI 2000 in College Park, Maryland

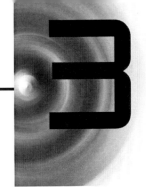

Sixteenth-Note Grooves

Gear needed for this chapter: kick, snare, hi-hat, and ride cymbal.

You can set up a drum kit with only these pieces to practice this section:

This chapter introduces grooves that integrate a ton of sixteenth notes. Because the tempo of jungle/drum 'n' bass is so fast, it is important to get comfortable playing all of the fragments before moving forward. The other thing to remember is to be as precise and consistent as possible. Even though these grooves are meant to be played at hyperspeed, don't forget to play them cleanly. If you are sloppy, the groove won't sound good and will not work. I would rather hear these exercises slow and clean rather than quick and sloppy. These fragments will give you the opportunity to polish up your sixteenths between your hands and feet.

Fragments Group B: Sixteenth-Note Fragments: One-Note

Fragments Group B: Sixteenth-Note Fragments: Two-Note

Fragments Group B: Sixteenth-Note Fragments: Three-Note

Fragments Group B: Sixteenth-Note Fragments: Four-Note

Sixteenth-Note Exercises: One Measure

The following exercises contain the same fragments you just practiced, so they should be familiar to play. Remember to approach each groove as a drum machine or loop. Watch the accents!

Examples: 1, 7, 11, 13, 25, 42, 48

Sixteenth-Note Exercises: One Measure (cont'd)

Sixteenth-Note Exercises: Two Measures

Practice Tip: Practice one beat at a time. For example: Play beat 1 and rest for beats 2, 3, and 4. Then add the next beat 1 + 2 and rest for beats 3 and 4, and so on. This will allow your brain and muscles to memorize the exercise faster.

Examples: 1, 9, 13, 15, 23, 29, 32, 35, 40

Sixteenth-Note Exercises: Two Measure (cont'd)

Sixteenth-Note Exercises: Two Measures (cont'd)

World's Fastest Drummer Event

West L.A. Music's first annual WFD Challenge

Receiving the Guinness certificate from Alice Moss,
Guinness World Attractions, Orlando, Florida

VH-1 was on hand filming my world-record attempt for
their show "Rock & Roll Record Breakers"

Craig Alan, Alice Moss, Boo McAfee, Me, and Ed Sargent at
Guinness World Records Experience in Orlando, Florida, 2000

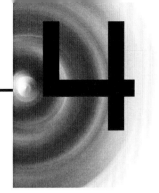

Basic Rolls and Buzzes

Gear needed for this chapter: kick, snare, hi-hat, and ride cymbal.
You can set up a drum kit with only these pieces to practice this section:

Rolls and buzzes are very important key elements that can be heard in jungle/drum 'n' bass music. In this chapter we will simulate these sounds by buzzing with the left hand on the snare drum. (If you are left-handed, use your right hand). Getting a really tight buzz roll is important since they are usually electronically produced for this style of music. Once again, these exercises will prepare you for the upcoming chapters. These exercises will get your hands doing something that they might not have done before. Be patient and remember to start slowly and work your way up to tempo only when comfortable.

Listening Tip: I recommend listening to as many jungle or drum 'n' bass CDs to study the sounds of different rolls created on drum machines and samplers. Once you have checked out the music, you can work on crescendos and decrescendos, which will add dynamics to your grooves.

CD-1 track 14

Fragments Group C: Buzz Fragments

Examples: C1, C4

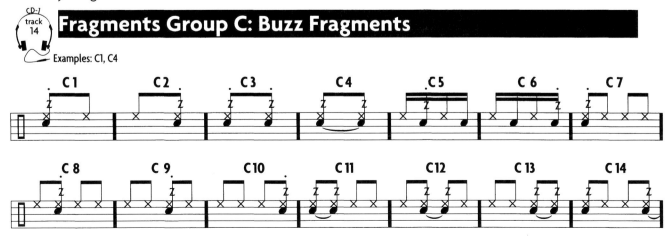

Buzz Warm-ups: One Measure

These exercises are designed to help you get familiar with playing the the short and long buzz strokes within a groove. Take it slowly and make sure there is a definite difference in sound between your short and long buzz strokes. Use the audio example CD for correct reference.

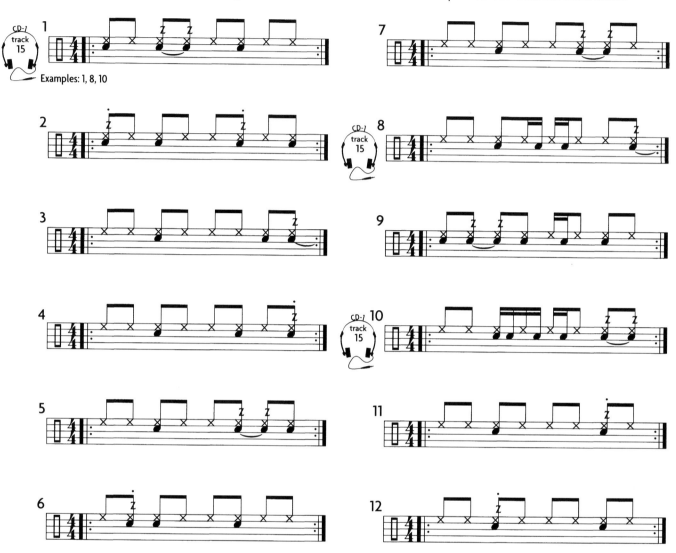

Buzz Warm-ups: Two Measures

Buzz Warm-ups: Two Measures (cont'd)

Buzz Exercises: One Measure

Practice Tip: If needed, practice each limb separately to get comfortable with each exercise.

Examples: 1, 8, 10, 13

Buzz Exercises: One Measure (cont'd)

Buzz Exercises: Two Measures

Buzz Exercises: Two Measures (cont'd)

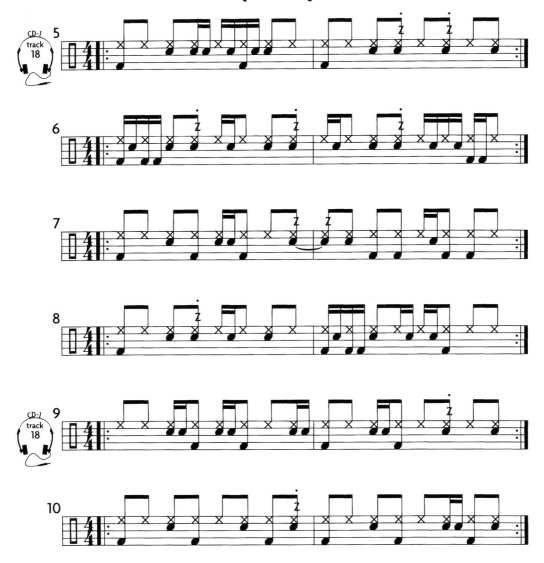

Buzz Cadences: Two Measures

Buzz cadences can be heard during breakdown sections of jungle/drum 'n' bass music. Most of the time the bass drum is not played, leaving almost a jungle march similar to a snare line cadence. The tricky part is keeping the hi-hat constant while performing the snare cadence.

60

Five-Stroke Roll

R R L L R   *or LLRRL sticking can be used

Five-Stroke Roll Warm-ups

Play these exercises slow and get comfortable moving from the snare drum to the hi-hat.

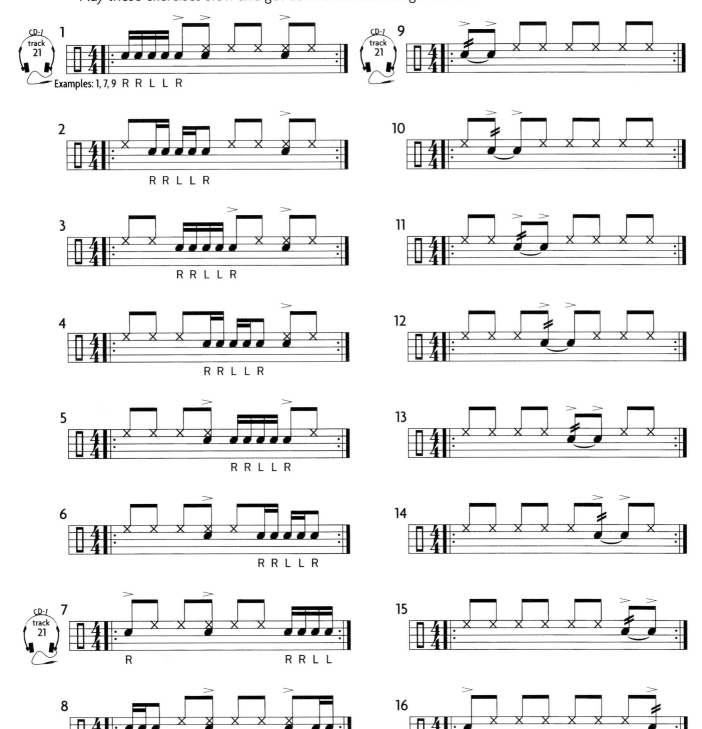

Five-Stroke Roll Exercises: One Measure

Be aware that you are now going to be performing multiple tasks. Take each exercise slowly and beware of new stickings and new movement!

Five-Stroke Roll Exercises: Two Measures

Five-Stroke Roll Exercises: Two Measures (cont'd)

Nine-Stroke Roll

Nine-Stroke Roll Warm-ups

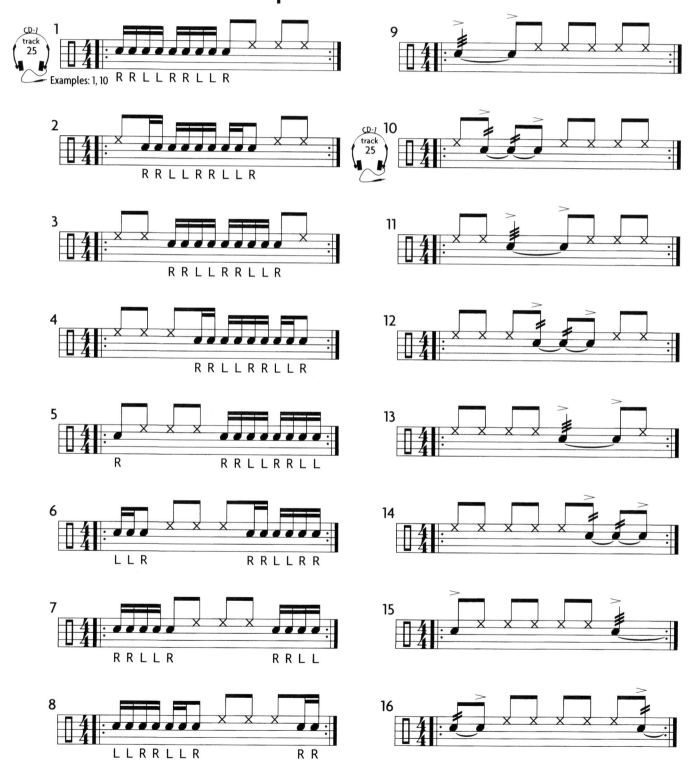

Nine-Stroke Roll Exercises: One Measure

Nine-Stroke Roll Exercises: Two Measures

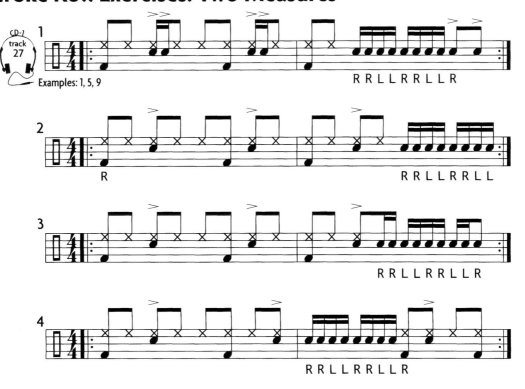

Nine-Stroke Roll Exercises: Two Measures (cont'd)

Five- and Nine-Stroke Roll Exercises: Two Measures with Buzzes

The following ten exercises put it all together. The goal is to have the rolls and buzzes become second nature in your playing. The more you practice, the more natural it will become. If needed, practice these exercises without the buzz strokes at first. Then when you're comfortable, add in the buzz strokes to complete the groove.

Five- and Nine-Stroke Roll Exercises: Two Measures (cont'd)

Demonstrating the Meinl "Rabb Pack" cymbal set in the Meinl
booth at the Frankfurt Musikmesse, 2001

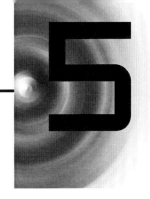

Unison Jungle

Gear needed for this chapter: kick, snare, hi-hat, and ride cymbal.

You can set up a drum kit with only these pieces to practice this section:

Unison: At the same time; at once.

In this chapter we will focus on playing two parts at the same time or in unison. The following exercises are one- and two-bar patterns where the hi-hat is playing in unison with either the bass drum or snare drum. First play each exercise as written. Then you may use a cowbell, tambourine, or different sound source instead of the hi-hat. This will allow you to expand and explore new sound options for each groove. Don't forget to start at a slow pace!

Practice Tip: When performing these exercises, try to play the two instruments in unison (precisely at the same time). The goal is to sound like one individual attack, not a flam. Practice hitting the hi-hat and snare/bass drum together S-L-O-W-L-Y to avoid flamming.

Fragments Group D: Unison Bass Drum Fragments

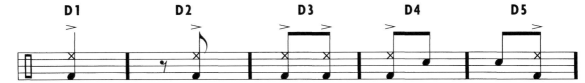

Unison Bass Drum Exercises: One Measure

Examples: 1, 10, 18, 21, 29, 42

70

Unison Bass Drum Exercises: One Measure (cont'd)

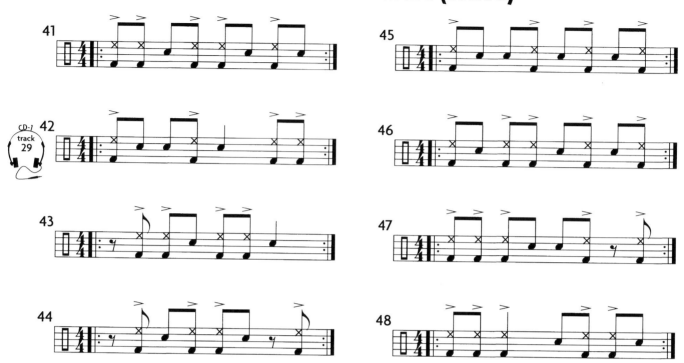

Unison Bass Drum Exercises: Two Measures

Remember that these exercises create a lot of open space within each measure. Try not to rush since the eighth notes normally providing a comfort zone are not being played.

Examples: 1, 3, 9, 15, 19, 23

Unison Snare Drum Exercises: Two Measures (cont'd)

Unison Bass Drum Exercises: Two Measures (cont'd)

Fragments Group E: Unison Snare Drum Fragments

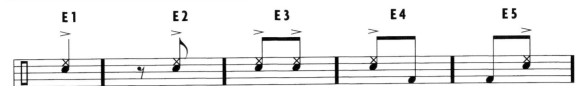

Unison Snare Drum Exercises: One Measure

These examples will feel different since the unison instruments have changed. Your main focus should be on playing the snare and hi-hat at precisely the same time. Remember to avoid flamming.

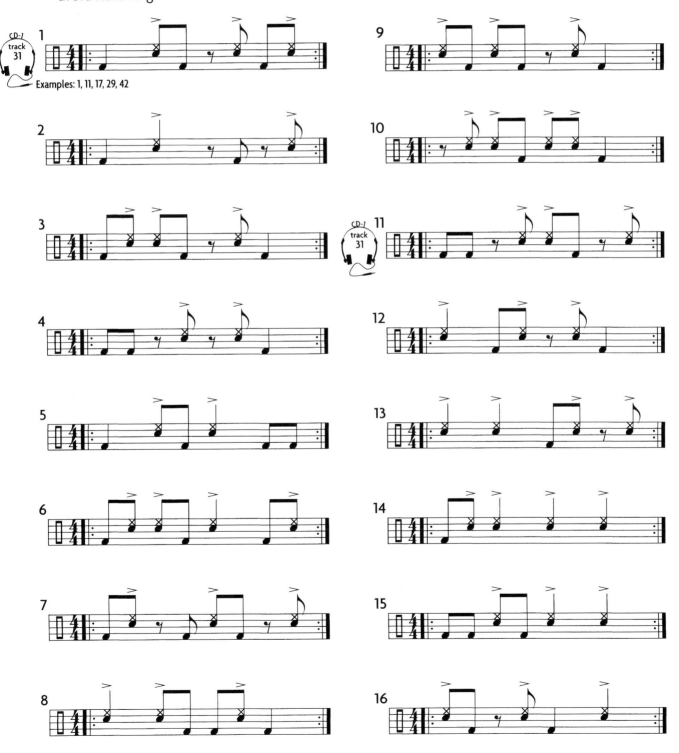

Examples: 1, 11, 17, 29, 42

Unison Snare Drum Exercises: One Measure (cont'd)

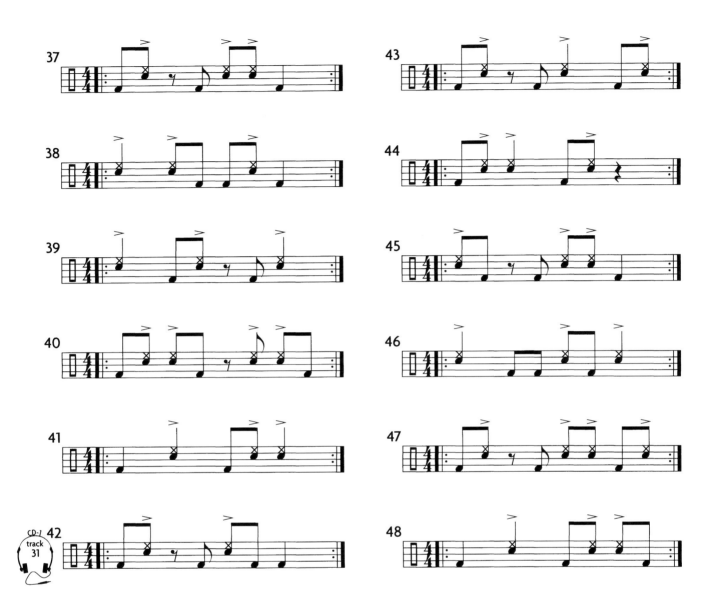

Unison Snare Drum Exercises: Two Measures

Examples: 1, 7, 13, 15, 19, 23

Unison Snare Drum Exercises: Two Measures (cont'd)

Fragments Group F: Unison Bass Drum Combinations

Unison Bass Drum Combination Exercises: One Measure

These exercises combine eighth- and sixteenth-note unison patterns. Any consecutive sixteenth notes can be a challenge. Remember to play cleanly and precisely.

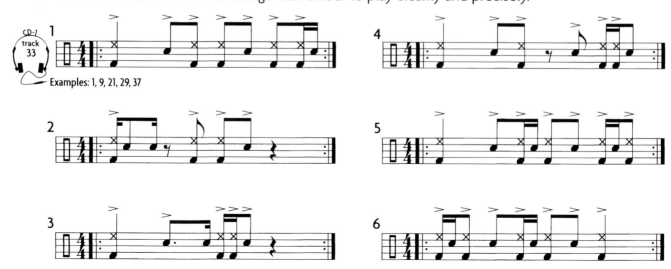

Examples: 1, 9, 21, 29, 37

Unison Bass Drum Combination Exercises: One Measure (cont'd)

Unison Bass Drum Combination Exercises: Two Measures

Examples: 1, 5, 7, 13, 19, 23

Unison Bass Drum Combination Exercises: Two Measures (cont'd)

Fragments Group G: Unison Snare Drum Combination Fragments

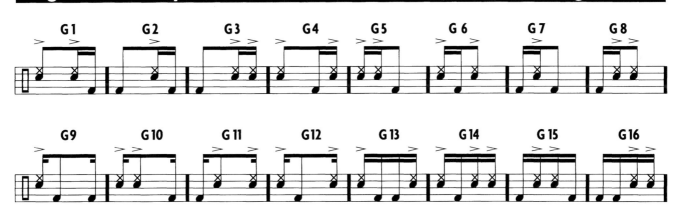

Unison Snare Drum Combination Exercises: One Measure

Practice all fragment exercises individually to get familiar with the note groupings.

86

Unison Snare Drum Combination Exercises: One Measure (cont'd)

Unison Snare Drum Combination Exercises: Two Measures

Examples: 1, 5, 11

Unison Snare Drum Combination Exercises: Two Measures (cont'd)

Linear Jungle Grooves

Gear needed for this chapter: kick, snare, hi-hat, and ride cymbal.
You can set up a drum kit with only these pieces to practice this section:

In this chapter we will focus on linear jungle grooves. In the following exercises, no two instruments are played at the exact same time. All of the notes are on separate planes. If you have studied linear funk patterns, then you will be very familiar with these exercises. It is important to practice the fragments first to become comfortable playing them by themselves before moving on. Once you're comfortable, begin practicing the exercises slowly and gradually speed up the tempo. Think of each exercise as a linear funk groove when practicing at a slow or medium tempo.

Practice Tip: Combine any four linear fragments to create your own original linear jungle grooves. Always use a drum machine or metronome to keep your time and groove solid!

Fragments Group H: Linear Eighth-Note Fragments

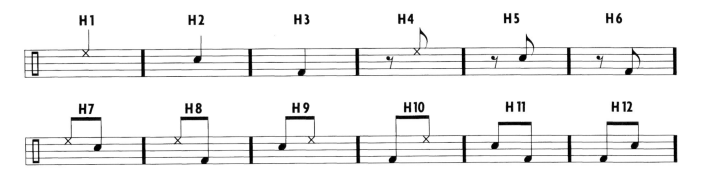

Linear Eighth-Note Exercises: One Measure

These exercises are harder than they look. They are basically fragments combined into grooves.
Try to remember that no two limbs are playing at the same time. Each note has an individual
place in which to be played. Take it slowly and become comfortable with each measure.

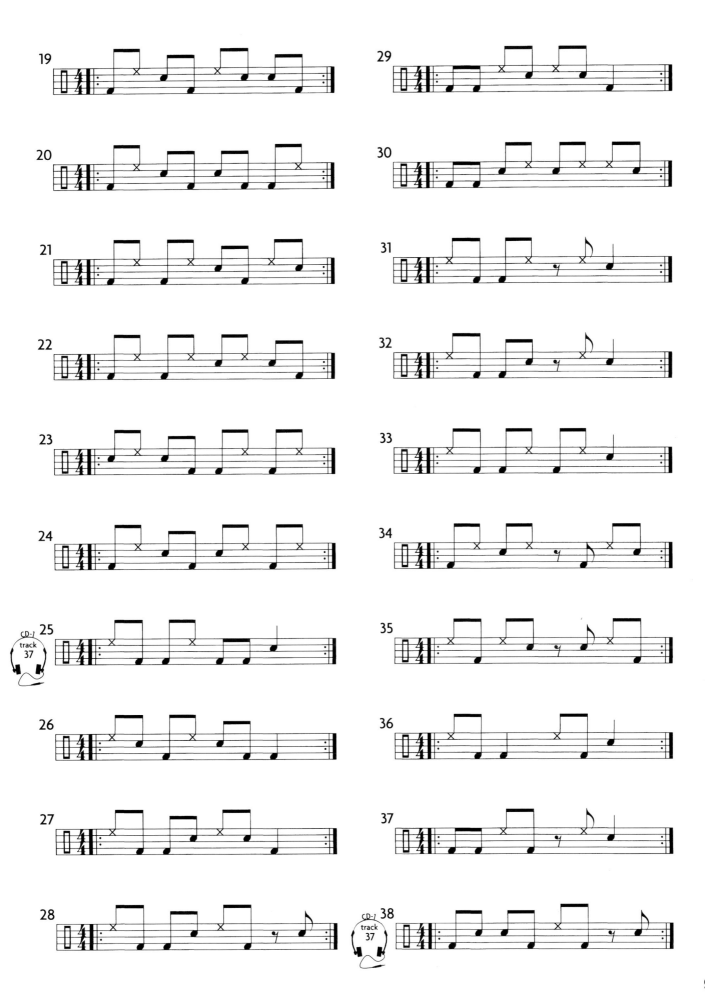

Linear Eighth-Note Exercises: One Measure (cont'd)

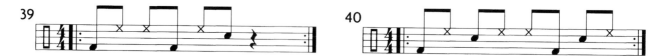

Linear Eighth-Note Exercises: Two Measures

Practice Tip: When you're practicing these exercises, try to do it one measure at a time. Then when you're comfortable, add the second measure and create the two-bar loop.

— Examples: 1, 5, 13, 19, 21, 25, 28

Linear Eighth-Note Exercises: Two Measures (cont'd)

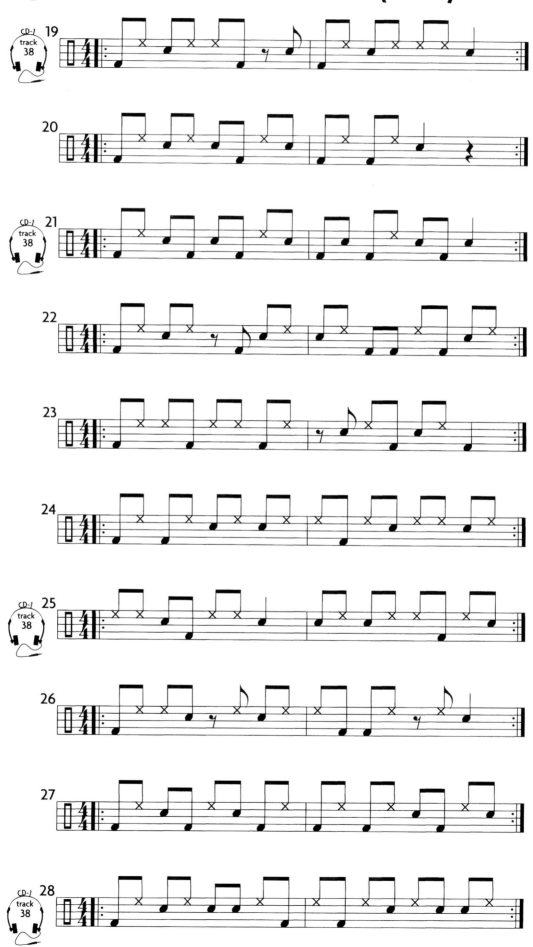

Fragments Group I: Linear Combinations—Three Notes

The fragments below should be played individually and then combined to create your own beats. Remember that these fragments also sound great slow as linear funk grooves.

Fragments Group I (cont'd): Linear Combinations—Four Notes

Linear Combination Exercises: One Measure

The following exercises utilize both eighth- and sixteenth-note fragments. These really begin to sound like the jungle/drum 'n' bass grooves that are heard at clubs, on albums, and on TV. Start to concentrate on the sound and feel you are creating on the drum set.

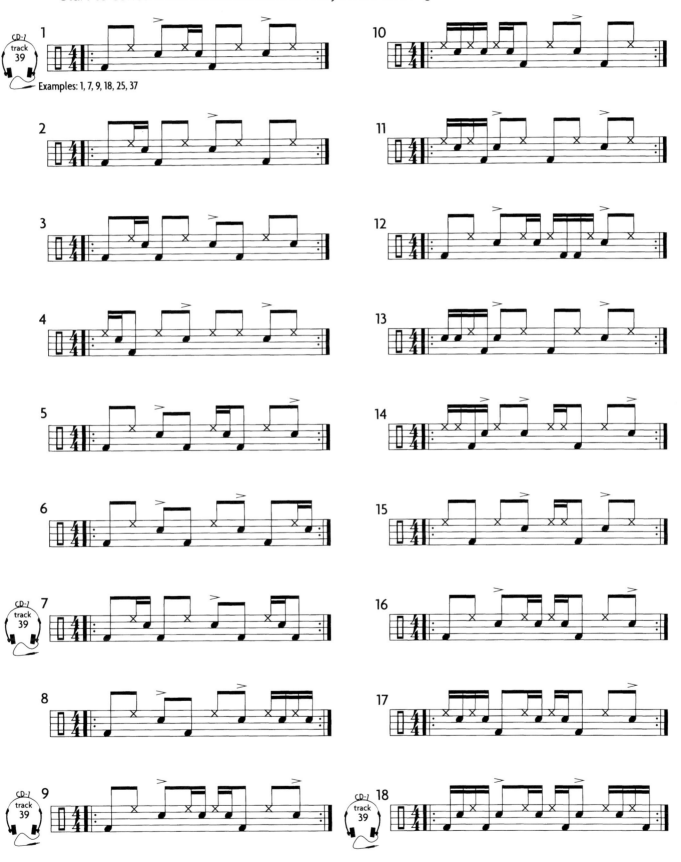

Examples: 1, 7, 9, 18, 25, 37

Linear Combination Exercises: One Measure (cont'd)

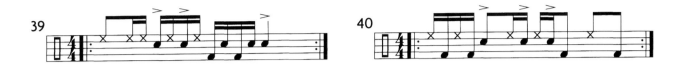

Linear Combination Exercises: Two Measures

Try to create a loop feel when practicing these exercises. Notice how the phrasing goes over the bar line in some of these grooves. It creates the illusion of playing an odd time pattern.

Examples: 1, 7, 14, 15, 19, 27

Linear Combination Exercises: Two Measures (cont'd)

Me and Zoro

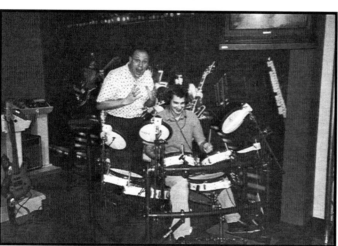

Dan Del Fiorentino and me

Thomas Pridgen, me, and Tony Royster Jr.

Marco Minnemann and me

Me and Johnny Craviotto

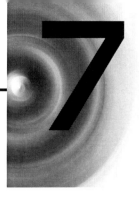

Hi-Hat Exercises

Gear needed for this chapter: kick, snare, hi-hat, and ride cymbal.

You can set up a drum kit with only these pieces to practice this section:

The following hi-hat techniques and exercises will expand your sound possibilities for all exercises throughout this book. To achieve the open hi-hat sound, strike the top hi-hat cymbal and lift your toe off the footboard. To achieve the closed hi-hat sound, keep your foot firmly on the footboard while you strike the top hi-hat cymbal. If you are familiar with opening the hi-hat for funk or rock grooves, you should be able to execute the following exercises. Start by practicing each exercise individually. Start slowly as usual!

Practice Tip: Master each hi-hat exercise by itself, and then choose a basic feel bar and play the hi-hat exercises on top.

Fragments Group J: Hi-Hat Opening Fragments

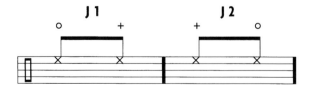

Preliminary Hi-Hat Exercise Feel Bars

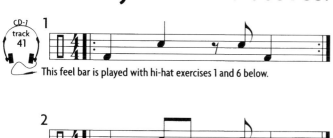

This feel bar is played with hi-hat exercises 1 and 6 below.

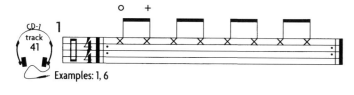

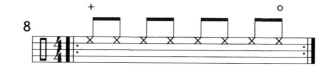

Hi-Hat Exercises

Examples: 1, 6

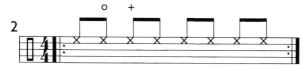

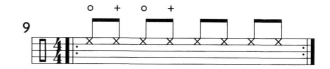

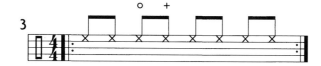

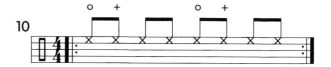

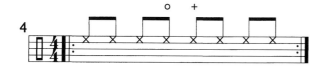

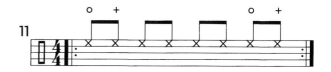

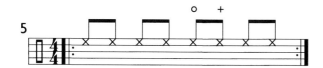

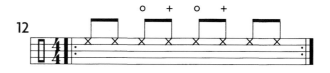

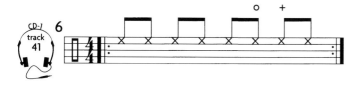

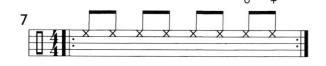

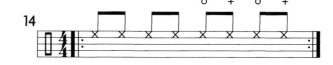

Hi-Hat Exercises (cont'd)

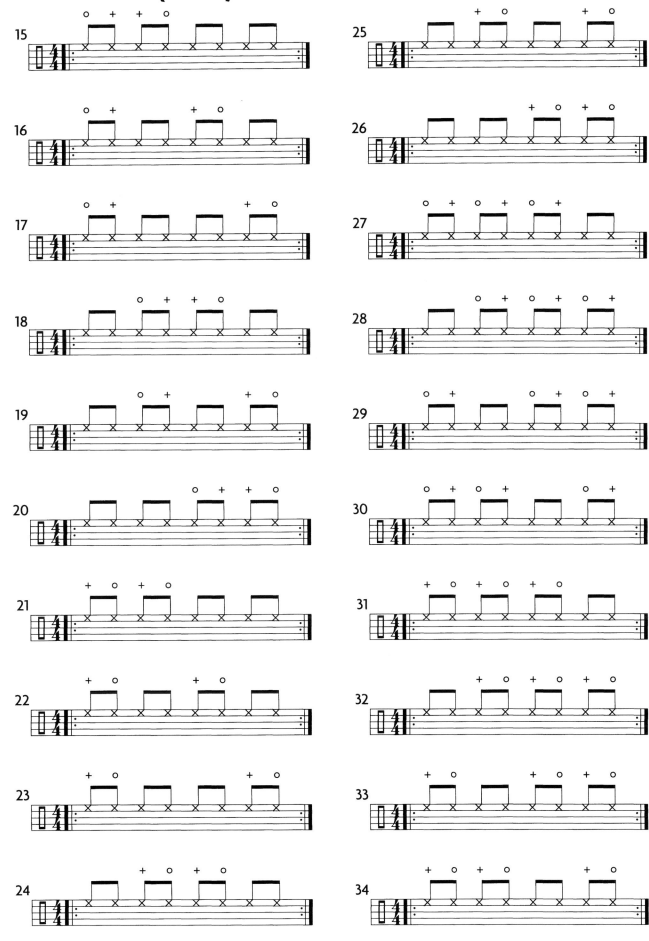

Hi-Hat Exercises (cont'd)

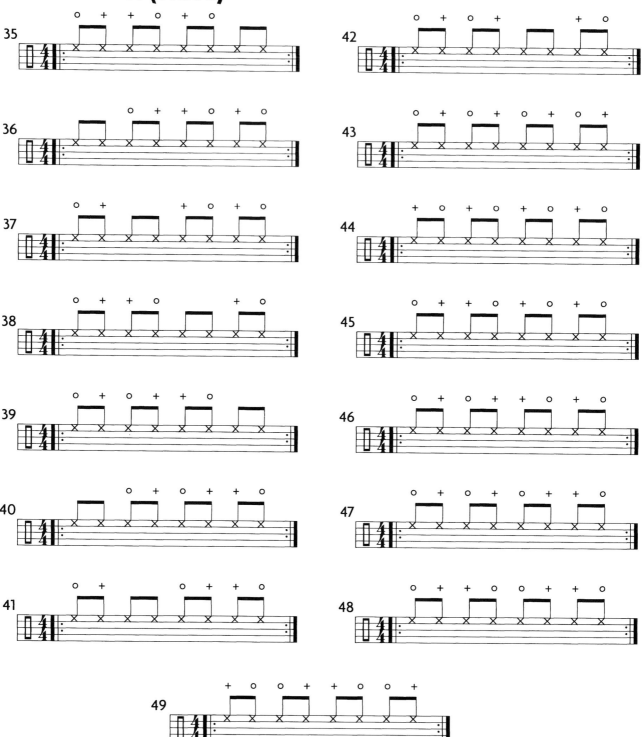

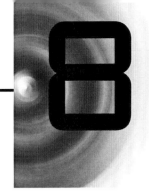

Multiple Snare Jungle Grooves.

Note: You should be comfortable with all of the exercises in the previous chapters before beginning this section.

Gear needed for this chapter: kick, snare, auxiliary snare-left, hi-hat, and ride cymbal. You can set up a drum kit with only these pieces to practice this section:

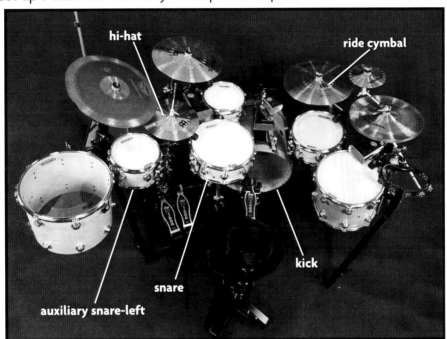

Since many different samples are used to create these high-energy grooves, it is necessary to use more than one snare drum. This will enable you to simulate the sampler by playing two snare sounds live and acoustically. Your hand will be required to move between your main snare and auxiliary snare. So, please don't be frustrated if this is your first time playing with two snare drums. Be patient and take your time on each exercise. Start slowly and get familiar with the motion between snares. Take your time and have fun!

Note: If you do not have an auxiliary snare, use another sound source such as a cowbell, tom, or tambourine. I suggest mounting the instrument to the left of the hi-hat (right of the hi-hat for left-handed players).

Listening Tip: Be sure to check out the audio example CD for an accurate reference. Remember that the circled notation is to be played on the auxiliary snare drum!

Multiple Snare Exercises: One Measure

Examples: 1, 13, 22, 25, 34

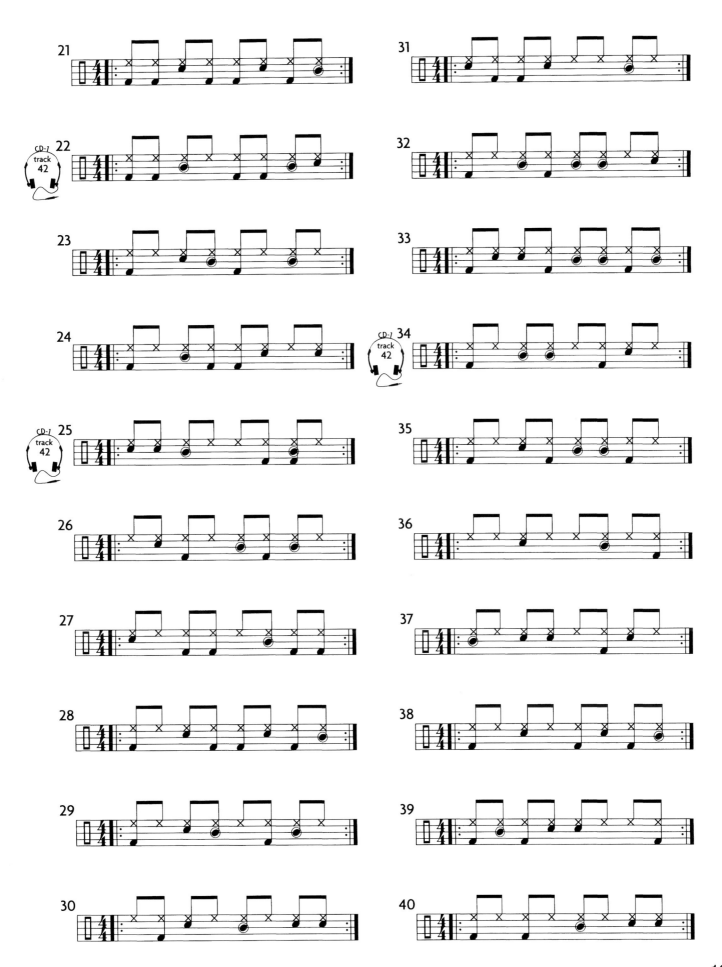

Multiple Snare Exercises: Two Measures

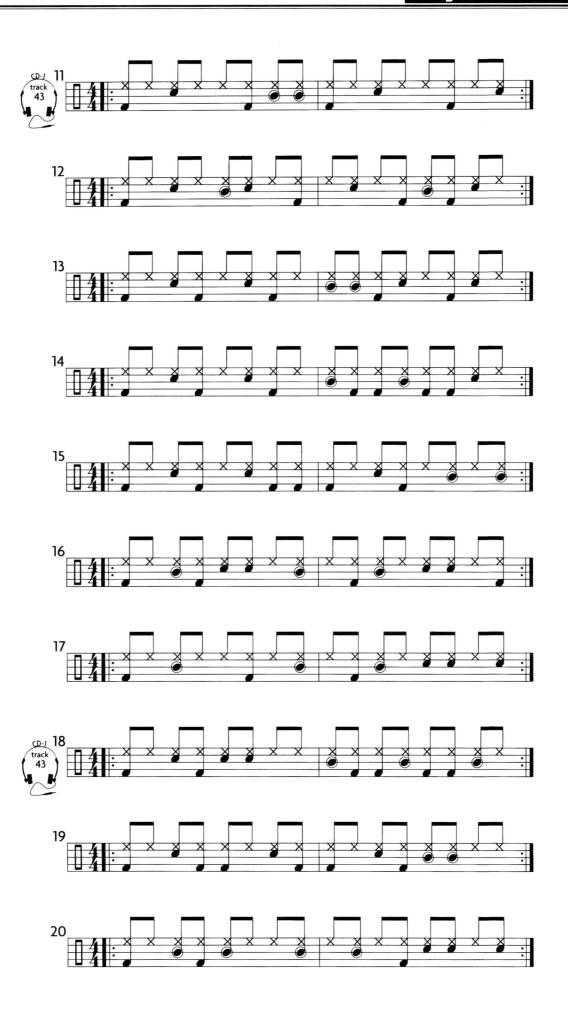

Multiple Snare Exercises: Two Measures (cont'd)

Multiple Snare Combination Exercises: One Measure

These exercises contain both eighth- and sixteenth-note fragments. Keep in mind that more notes usually means more challenging. Be sure to look out for the circled auxiliary snare notes. Take it slowly!

Examples: 1, 13, 29, 37

Multiple Snare Combination Exercises: One Measure (cont'd)

Multiple Snare Combination Exercises: Two Measures

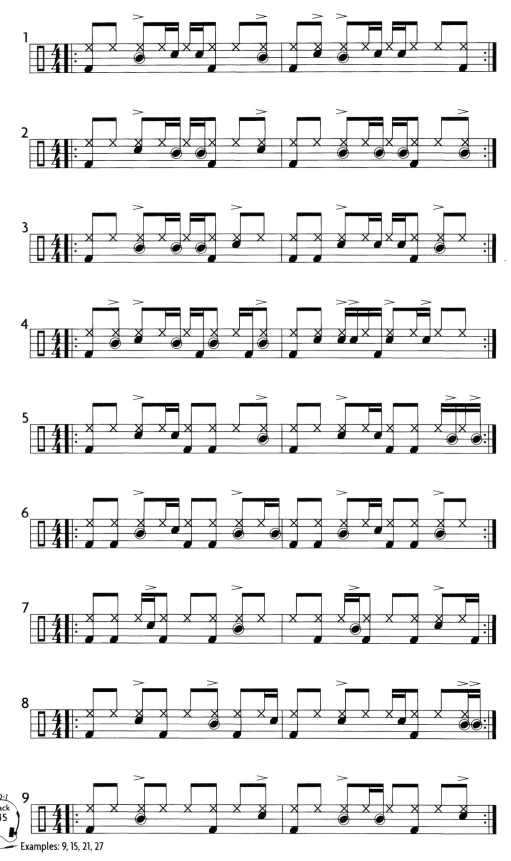

Examples: 9, 15, 21, 27

115

Multiple Snare Combination Exercises: Two Measures (cont'd)

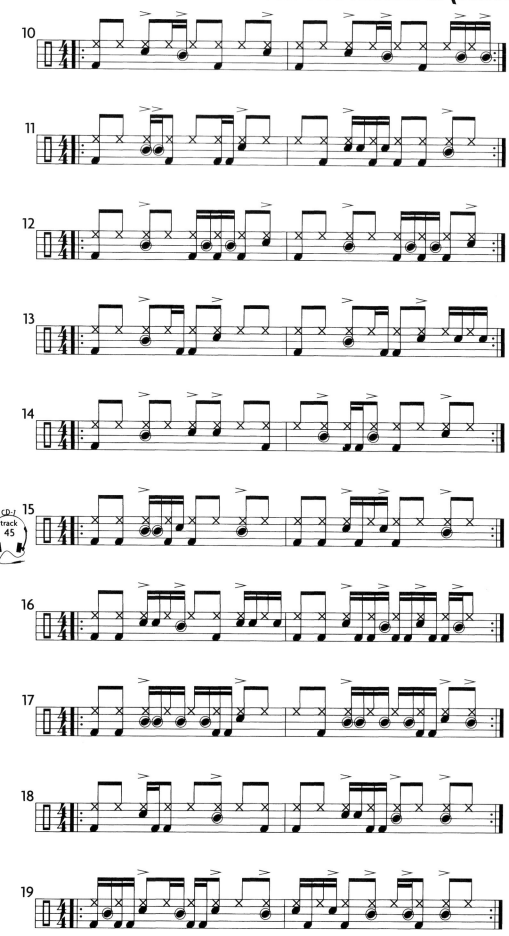

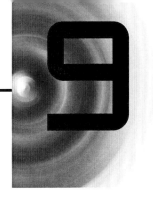

Split Grooves

Gear needed for this chapter: kick, snare, auxiliary snare-left, hi-hat, and ride cymbal. You can set up a drum kit with only these pieces to practice this section:

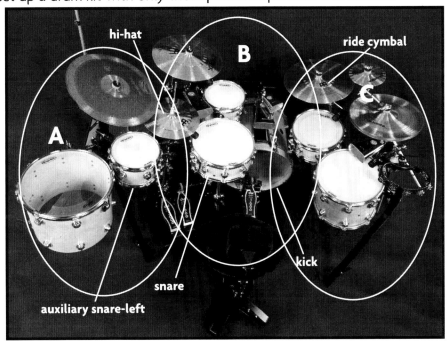

Because of the programmed nature of jungle/drum 'n' bass grooves, you will hear the drum set change throughout each song. To make this possible in a live situation, it is important to practice switching up the sounds of the drum set. The following exercises will allow you to get familiar with splitting up your drum set. It is my version of being a human drum machine or sampler. I virtually split up my drum set into three different drum sets. (See Johnny's Split-Kit diagram below). This enables me to cut up my grooves as a programmer would. Practice each exercise individually and get familiar with the motion between hi-hat/main snare and ride/auxiliary snare. There is even more movement in this chapter, so remember to take it slowly until you're comfortable.

Johnny's Split-Kit Diagram

NOTE: Main Bass Drum is applied to all three kits—A,B, and C
A=(Main Bass Drum), Hand Bass Drum, Auxiliary Snare Left, Flat Ride, Hi-Hat
B=(Main Bass Drum), Hi-Hat, Main Snare, Crash Cymbal, Rack Tom, Cowbells, Ride Cymbal, Auxiliary Snare Right
C=(Main Bass Drum), Ride Cymbal, Auxiliary Snare Right, Splash and China Cymbals, Floor Tom, Cowbells, Tambourine

Practice Tip: Check out any jungle or drum 'n' bass CD and listen for split grooves. Once you are familiar with a track, try to play along and simulate the groove on your own split-kit!

For the following set of exercises be sure to listen to the audio example CD to hear how these exercises should sound. Remember that the first measure uses the main snare drum and the second measure uses the auxiliary snare.

Split-Groove Exercises: Eighth-Note Combinations
Two-measure patterns switching sound sources every measure

Split-Groove Exercises: Sixteenth-Note Combinations
Two-measure patterns switching sound sources every measure

121

Split-Groove Exercises: Eighth-Note Combinations
Two-measure patterns switching sound sources on beats 3 and 4 of the second measure

Note: Be aware that the motion is much faster between snare drums since the sound sources switch on beats 3 and 4.

122

Split-Groove Exercises: Sixteenth-Note Combinations

Two-measure patterns switching sound sources on beats 3 and 4 of the second measure

Split-Groove Exercises: Eighth-Note Combinations
One-measure patterns switching sound sources every two beats

Split-Groove Exercises: Eighth- and Sixteenth-Note Combinations
One-measure patterns switching sound sources every two beats

Ostinato Grooves

Gear needed for this chapter: kick, snare, auxiliary snare-left, hi-hat, and ride cymbal.
You can set up a drum kit with only these pieces to practice this section:

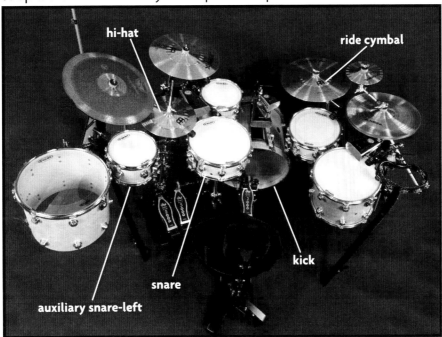

This chapter is definitely a coordination challenge. The goal is to create layered grooves by combining the basic feel bar with the auxiliary snare fills. Your right hand will play the hi-hat and main snare drum for the basic feel. Your left hand plays snare fills on the auxiliary snare drum. Practice the ostinatos first and then add in the basic feel bar. It is very important to start slowly so you can get yourself coordinated before increasing the tempo.

Practice Tip: Break down each measure into quarter-note sections to get familiar with each exercise. Don't forget to use a metronome or drum machine!

Basic Ostinato Grooves

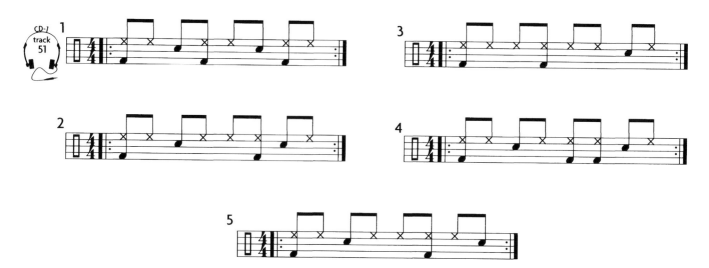

Eighth-Note Auxiliary Snare Fills

When practicing auxiliary snare fills on top of basic ostinato grooves, first play just the hi-hat and both snare parts. When you're comfortable, add the bass drum pattern to complete the groove.

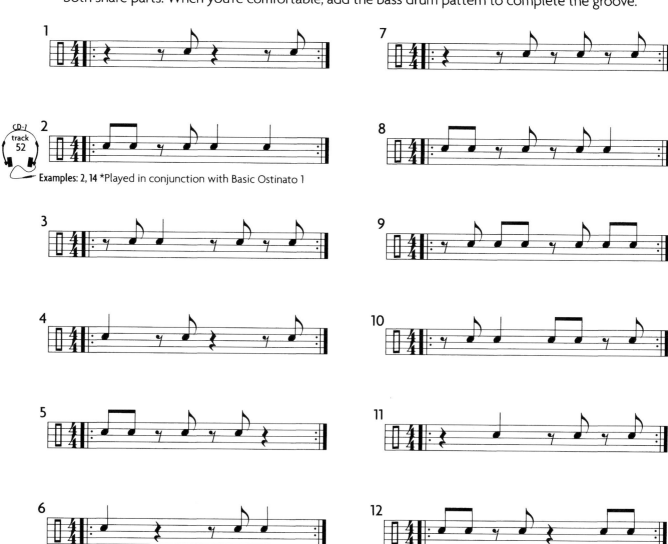

Examples: 2, 14 *Played in conjunction with Basic Ostinato 1

Eighth-Note Auxiliary Snare Fills (cont'd)

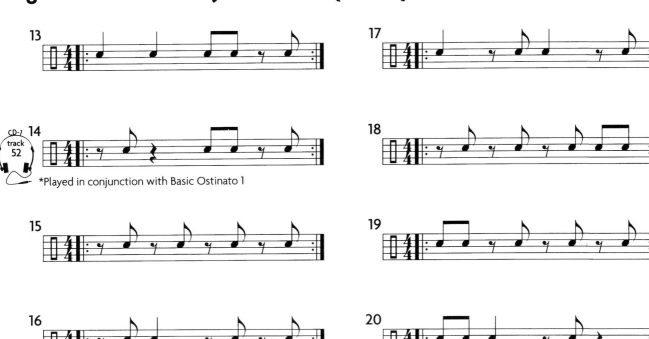

*Played in conjunction with Basic Ostinato 1

Eighth- and Sixteenth-Note Auxiliary Snare Fills

Examples: 1, 13 *Played in conjunction with Basic Ostinato 1

Eighth- and Sixteenth-Note Auxiliary Snare Fills (cont'd)

*Played in conjunction with Basic Ostinato 1

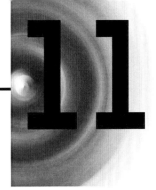

Double-Bass Jungle Grooves

Gear needed for this chapter: kick, snare, double-bass drum pedal, hi-hat, and ride cymbal. You can set up a drum kit with only these pieces to practice this section:

I n some cases you will hear multiple bass drum attacks in jungle/drum 'n' bass grooves. Many are possible to execute with only one foot, but some require the use of double-bass. The following exercises should be practiced using alternate strokes with your feet as notated.

Note: These exercises are written with the assumption that you have basic double-bass technique under control. If you are not familiar with playing two bass drums or a double pedal, I suggest you study some double-bass basics. There are many books and videos available to get your feet under control.

Practice Tip: Remember to alternate your feet. When performing sixteenth notes, you should either play them RLRL or LRLR, always alternating each foot stroke.

Preliminary Exercises

Play each exercise precisely and remember that we are simulating machine-style grooves.
Don't kill the bass drum parts. Play with authority; however, be sure not to overdo it!

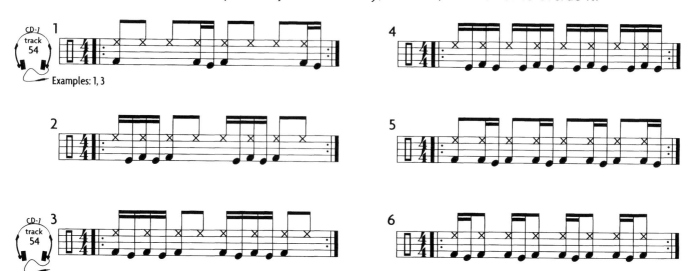

Eighth- and Sixteenth-Note Exercises: One Measure

Eighth- and Sixteenth-Note Exercises: Two Measures

MEINL Cymbal Company, Neustadt, Germany, 2001

Me and Norbert Saemann at the MEINL factory

*Me and Norbert in the MEINL cymbal vault
with my new Safari cymbal*

Udo Heubeck, me, and Norbert Saemann

Me, Reinhold Meinl, and Norbert Saemann

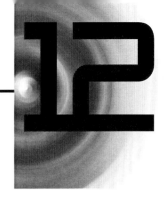

Transcriptions

Gear needed for this chapter: Ears, speakers or headphones, turntable or CD player, and various jungle/drum 'n' bass recordings.

These transcriptions are taken from recordings of grooves from various artists. I am a big fan of both programmed and live jungle/drum 'n' bass drumming. Even though I have showcased only one live drummer, remember that there are many other live jungle/drum 'n' bass drummers to check out. I have learned the most from listening, and I want to stress that along with practicing the physical exercises, listening to albums by different jungle/drum 'n' bass artists will enhance your understanding of the music. I assure you that listening will become your reference and guide to what this amazing music is all about!

Transcription 1: DJ Goldie – "Manslaughter" (programmed drum track)

Goldie was the first drum 'n' bass artist I was turned on to. This track contains a very catchy and syncopated drum groove. Be sure to check out other albums by Goldie!

Transcription 2: Origin Unknown – "Valley of the Shadows" (programmed drum track)

This particular track is harder than it looks. The tempo is extremely fast. When I first heard this groove, I found that beats 3 and 4 are what gave me a challenge. Take it slowly and really play it precisely. Once you increase the tempo, you will see what I mean!

Transcription 3: PFM – "Wash Over Me" (programmed drum track)

This groove really has a great trashy hi-hat/cymbal choke on the "and" of 4. I usually practice this one first using an open and closed hi-hat. Then when I am warmed up, I substitute the hi-hat with a cymbal choke. Don't kill yourself!
Groove A: basic feel; Groove B: basic feel with hi-hat or cymbal choke.

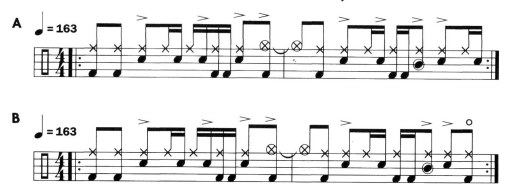

Transcription 4: Jungle Warfare Vol. 3 – "Standard Amen" (programmed drum track)

This transcription is taken from the Jungle Warfare sampling CD. It is extremely challenging to play all the notes accurately and precisely. This is a fantastic warm-up exercise and should be started slowly to ensure proper groove and feel.

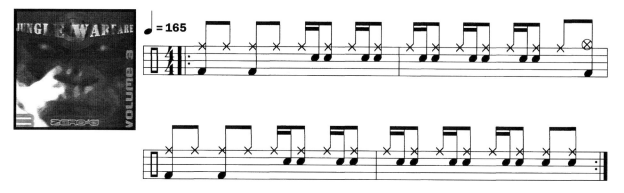

Transcription 5: Jungle Warfare Vol. 3 – "Scotti Bk" (programmed drum track)

This is another groove transcribed off of the Jungle Warfare sampling CD. It has the best of all worlds. It creates the stop-start effect on the drum set. It is the perfect groove to simulate on the drum set. Notice the hi-hat part played with the foot. This is played by closing the hats using the footboard of the hi-hat stand. Remember to start slowly!

Transcription 6: Soul Coughing (El Oso) – "Rolling" (Yuval Gabay—live drums)

Here is an excellent example of a drummer performing drum 'n' bass live. The groove is similar to the exercises found in Chapter 3. I recommend that you check out this album. It is not entirely drum 'n' bass-oriented; however, Soul Coughing is a killer group.

Transcription 7: Soul Coughing (El Oso) – "Blame" (Yuval Gabay—live drums)

In this example, Yuval does a great job simulating the electronic sounds of drum 'n' bass. It is a basic groove but has an amazing feel. This groove demonstrates how a standard eighth-note pattern can be enhanced by playing a tambourine stick in the right hand.

*See Advanced Sound Exercises for a full explanation on the jingle stick.

Transcription 8: Soul Coughing (El Oso) – "$300" (Yuval Gabay—live drums)

Once again, Yuval uses a tambourine stick in his right hand, which creates sixteenths on top of the groove. Check it out!

Transcription 9: Soul Coughing (El Oso) – "$300" solo (Yuval Gabay—live drums)

In this solo break, Yuval plays a tambourine stick and really keeps this solo very syncopated. When practicing this transcription example, break down each measure slowly before moving up to tempo.

Practice Tip: Listen like CRAZY! Just like learning any other style, the best way to learn this style is to immerse yourself in the music. Buy as many jungle and/or drum 'n' bass records as you can. The more you hear it and play along with it, the more you will understand the vocabulary. Remember that compilation records of various artists give you more bang for your buck! The Internet is a great way to check out jungle/drum 'n' bass at little or no cost. (See Discography and Webography.)

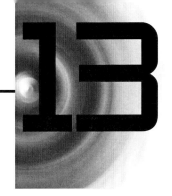

Advanced Sound Exercises

Gear needed for this chapter: Go extreme! Play whatever you have. Be creative, but remember to stay musical!

Accessories needed for this chapter: MEINL Jingle Stick, MEINL Johnny Rabb Drumbals, johnnyraBB RhythmSaws, and a cowbell.

Snare-Muting Exercises

Snare-muting exercises are designed to dampen the snare head and simulate machine or programmed grooves. The butt of the stick in your right hand will rest on the snare drum head (see photo on next page). When eighth notes are played on the hi-hat, you will achieve a combination sound of hi-hat and muted snare drum. Backbeats should be played with the left hand on the open section of the snare drum. First listen to the audio example track and then work through the exercises.

CD-1 track 57

Examples: 1, 2

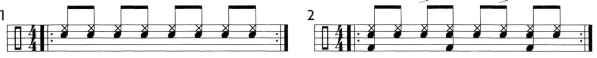

Practice Tip: After listening to the audio example CD, Go back through all of the exercises using the snare-muting technique.

Snare Chatter Exercises

Snare chatter exercises use the same hand position as the snare-muting exercises. The goal is to create sixteenth notes on the snare drum with the butt end of the stick. Your palm should be resting on the snare drum head. While playing eighth notes on the hi-hat, the butt of the stick should rebound up and down, creating sixteenth notes on the snare drum. The end result is eighth notes on the hi-hat and sixteenth notes on the snare drum. The left hand will play the backbeats on the open side of the snare drum.

CD-1 track 58

Examples: 1, 2 (improvisation)

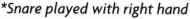

Snare played with right hand

Practice Tip: Listen to the audio example CD to understand the sound of the snare chatter. Don't get frustrated; use the photos to make sure you are in the correct playing position.

Sixteenth-Note Exercises Using the Tip and Butt End of the Stick

Because jungle/drum 'n' bass grooves are played at such fast tempos, it was necessary to find a way to play sixteenth notes on the hi-hat or ride cymbal. The following exercises use the tip and butt end of the stick. The tip will play all eighth notes—1 & 2 & 3 & 4 &—while the butt end will play all the e's and a's. The easiest way to get started is to choke up slightly on your grip, and then play eighth notes with a normal stroke. While doing this, look at the end of the stick. You will notice the butt end will be playing the e's and a's in the air. Next, move the stick across the hi-hat. Make sure you place the stick on either side of the hi-hat clutch. Now play the eighth notes on the backside of the hi-hat and the e's and a's on the edge of the hi-hat closest to you. (See photo next page.)

CD-1 track 59

Examples: 1, 4 (improvisation)

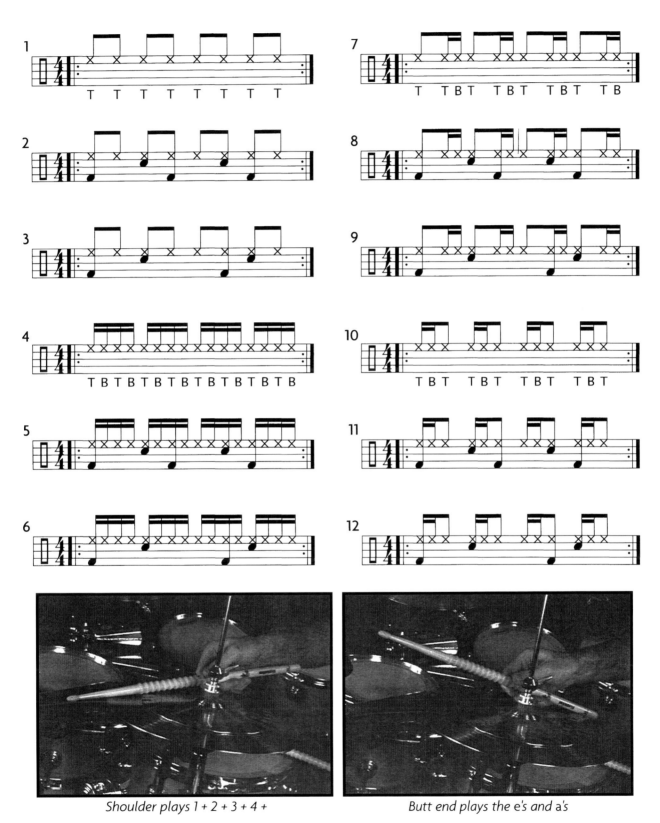

Shoulder plays 1 + 2 + 3 + 4 +

Butt end plays the e's and a's

Practice Tip: When practicing these exercises, do not try to force a stroke from the butt end of the stick. It should happen almost automatically as a rebound preparing for the next eighth-note stroke.

Sixteenth-Note Cowbell Exercises

This next exercise is something I have found that works very well for creating even sixteenth notes in the cowbell. First place the tip and shoulder of the stick in the mouth of the cowbell. (See photo.) To get a feel for basic movement, simply move the stick up and down inside the bell. The next thing to do is use it in a groove. All downstrokes will create your eighth notes and the up-strokes will create the *e*'s and *a*'s.

CD-1 track 60

Examples: 1 (improvisation)

Downstroke

Upstroke

Practice Tip: Concentrate on the downstroke eighth notes being your timekeeper. This way your sixteenth notes will fall into the groove. Check out the audio example CD to see how it should sound and feel. Definitely start slowly until you are comfortable.

Cymbal Choke Exercises

Cymbal choking is often heard in jungle/drum 'n' bass drum grooves. Below are some simple exercises to get you started. If you have never attempted to choke a cymbal, please take it slowly. Refer to the photos on the next page and notice the way the stick is being held in the left hand (choking hand). The cymbal should be grabbed using the thumb on top of the cymbal and the index finger on the bottom of the cymbal. The right hand strikes the cymbal while the left hand chokes it. Practice this VERY SLOWLY!

WARNING: Do not attempt any cymbal chokes if your cymbal is cracked or broken in any way. This can cause serious injury to your hands. Remember that you need your hands. I will not be responsible if you rip off a nail, cut your hand, or even slice off your head! Believe me, I have had my share of cymbals under my index fingernail. (IT HURTS!) PLEASE BE CAREFUL!

CD-1 track 61

Examples: audio description

Practice Tip: After completing the exercises, go back to the beginning of the book and try to choke the cymbal on the downbeat (beat 1 of each measure). When proficient with this add cymbal chokes anywhere you desire to spice up your grooves.

Drumbals

Drumbals are cymbals that were designed to be played on drums. I developed these instruments with the MEINL cymbal company. They are perfect for imitating white noise, hand claps, and other electronic effects. I believe the Drumbals transform your acoustic drum set into an acoustic drum machine. Be sure to listen to the audio examples CD to hear musical applications of the Drumbal.

CD-1
track
62

Examples: audio description

Jingle Stick Exercises

Using my MEINL jingle stick allows me to create sixteenth notes at the same time I am playing eighth notes on the hi-hat. Hold the jingle stick in your right hand and play eighth notes
on the hi-hat as you normally would. You will notice that on the way back to hit the next
eighth note, the halt will cause the jingle stick to play the *e*'s and *a*'s. Another way to look at
it is to play the jingle stick like a standard tambourine. First play sixteenth notes and then
simply play eighth notes on the hi-hat.

Examples: 1, 2

Practice Tip: Once you get comfortable playing sixteenth notes with the jingle stick, go to
the beginning of the book and play all of the eighth-note exercises with the jingle stick. It
will create a whole new feel for each exercise!

**WARNING: The jingle stick will give you a workout since it has a
thicker handle. This can cause cramping in your hand if your chops
aren't up to par. If this is a new exercise for you, I advise that you
build up your stamina before going nuts!**

The RhythmSaw

I developed RhythmSaws for simulating DJ scratches, Latin effects, and nearly endless sound possibilities. You can experiment on cowbells, woodblocks, tambourines, rims, hi-hats, and drums. Check out the audio example CD to hear how RhythmSaws can enhance your playing. Be sure to check out the *RhythmSaw Techniques* video available from johnnyraBB Publications (www.johnnyrabb.com).

CD-1 track 64

Examples: audio description

Practice Tip: Open your mind and have fun with RhythmSaws. You can't play them wrong!

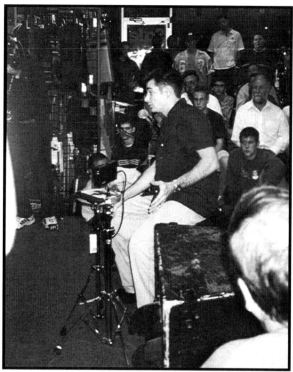

*Demonstrating the Drumometer during a clinic
at Columbus Pro Percussion in 2000*

*Teaching the Freehand Technique to a class
at KOSA 2001 in Castleton, Vermont*

Talking to fans following a clinic in Nantes, France

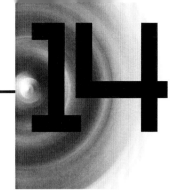

Freehand Technique

Gear needed for this chapter: kick, snare, hi-hat, and ride cymbal.
You can set up a drum kit with only these pieces to practice this section:

The freehand technique allows you to play quick rhythms with one hand that would normally be played with two. This chapter focuses on this technique that I have developed using the rim as the fulcrum. For a full explanation on how to perform this method, please check out *The Freehand Technique* book/DVD soon to be released by Warner Bros. Publications.

Listening Tip: Take a listen to the audio example CD to hear how the freehand technique can open new doors for your playing. It allows you to keep the eighth-note hi-hat pattern constant as sixteenth notes are performed with one hand on the snare drum.

One-Measure Examples

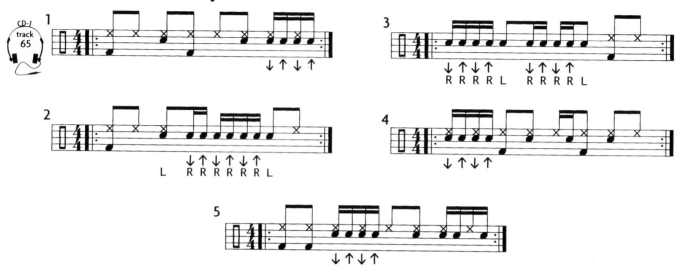

Two-Measure Examples

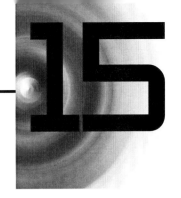

Basic Electronics

This section will give you a basic foundation and understanding of basic electronics. I perform with all of the equipment listed below. Roland electronics are user-friendly and an easy way to dive into electronics for either live or recorded performance.

Please listen to the audio example CD for examples and basic instruction to get a better understanding of how these instruments work.

 Boss DR-303 (Phrase Sampler) – A phrase sampler is a sort of digital recorder that will capture sounds or grooves that can be played back by pressing one of its eight pads. This piece of equipment allows me to cut up my own grooves or record a sample from an outside source. From there I can create my own original music.

Boss DR-303

 Roland SPD-20 (Pad Controller) – This controller is very simple and fun to use. Just by plugging it in, you can perform on many different preset drum sets. It is capable of triggering external sound sources via MIDI. A hi-hat trigger pedal and bass drum trigger pedal allow you to play this just like a drum set. It is great for quiet practice or live/studio performance. All of the audio examples use the SPD-20's internal sounds. They work great for jungle/drum 'n' bass grooves.

 Roland HandSonic HPD-15 (Pad Controller) – The HandSonic was designed to be played with your hands. It has a ton of

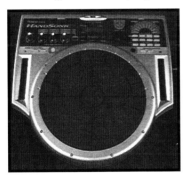 internal sounds including world percussion, drum-set sounds, special effects, bass, synth, and even bird calls. This tool alone can sound exactly like a programmed jungle/drum 'n' bass groove. By plugging in a hi-hat trigger pedal and bass drum trigger pedal, you can play it like a drum set. It also has the ability to control outside sound sources via MIDI and has a built-in sequencer and preset groove patterns. You can either write your own grooves or practice along with the presets. Play this by itself or make it part of your acoustic drum set.

Roland SPD-20

Hybrid drum sets give you the best of both worlds. Using the acoustic drum set along with either the HandSonic or SPD-20 will open your mind to new creative sound options.

Roland HandSonic

Hybrid Drum Setup – Acoustic drum set with Roland HandSonic HPD-15. (See Photo A.)

Hybrid Drum Setup – acoustic drumset with Roland HandSonic HPD-15 and Roland SPD-20. (See Photo B.)

Writing tools are so important for all of us to have. I urge any drummer to pick up an instrument other than just the drums. If you are unfamiliar with melody, chords, harmony, and theory, you should try to learn about all of it. Learning to play many other instruments besides the drums allowed me the freedom to read and compose music. Below are examples of some basic equipment that is simple to operate and full of wonderful sounds.

Photo A

Roland PMA-5 – This personal music assistant is fantastic

for travel, vacation, and general portability. I am able to compose no matter where I am! It comes with an adapter and also runs on AA batteries if needed. It is fantastic for plane trips!

Photo B

Roland PMA-5

Roland MC-505 – The groovebox is killer! If you like the sounds of the Groove Loops CD, then you will love this piece of gear. It has grooves ranging from jungle, drum 'n' bass, hip-hop, house, you name it. It also is a fantastic way for me to compose my original jungle/drum 'n' bass music. All of my tracks were recorded using the MC-505's internal sounds. Investing in a good drum machine is important for practicing. Another inexpensive and user-friendly drum machine is the Boss Dr. Rhythm (DR-202). This machine is perfect to use while practicing.

Roland MC-505

The MadPlayer™ from MadWaves™ puts you in total control

of the music. MadPlayer creates copyright-free music you can change to make uniquely your own with the simple touch of a button, in 20 of today's hot music styles. The music is always brand new. Every single time. You pick the style. MadPlayer creates the song. The MadPlayer also is an MP3 player and FM radio!

MadPlayer

Putting It All Together

This final chapter provides you with audio examples to listen to jungle/drum 'n' bass grooves in a musical context. This is the real application of all of the techniques that you have just studied. When dealing with the history of jungle/drum 'n' bass, there seems to be a series of unwritten rules. In my view, these rules are meant to be broken in order to develop your own style and approach to this music. My idea is to take any form or style of music and apply jungle/drum 'n' bass grooves to create my own hybrid musical style. That is why I call this chapter *Putting It All Together*. Check out audio example CD 2 to hear some of my ideas; then work on creating your own grooves while playing along with Tracks 7–13, the groove loops.

 Track 1 - Basic Electronics

 Track 2 - Roland SPD-20 Example

 Track 3 - Roland HandSonic Example

 Track 4 - Roland SPD-20 Hybrid Drum Set Example

 Track 5 - Breaking the Rules

 Track 6 - Gap Track - from Johnny Rabb's Jungle/Drum 'n' Bass
Solo Album *Acoustic Machine*, available from johnnyraBB
Publications (www.johnnyrabb.com)

 Tracks 7–13 - Groove Loops

Appendix

Suggested Listening

The listening guide below will get you started developing a collection of jungle/drum 'n' bass music. These are just a few of the many artisits out there for you to check out. To get going, you can't go wrong buying recordings by Roni Size, LTJ Bukem, and DJ Goldie.

ARTIST	LABEL	ARTIST/PRODUCER
Source Direct	Metal Headz/Science	Source Direct
DJ Zine	Ganja Kru	Published: True Playaz
DJ Hype	Ganja Kru	Published: True Playaz
The Riddler	Joker	Bizzy B & Pugwash
The Dynamic Duo	Joker	Dynamic Duo
The Dream Team	Joker	Bizzy B & Pugwash
Rudebwoy Monty	Frontline	Monty
Pascal	Suburban Base	Pascal/Johnny Jungle
Emerald Cricket	Jungle Sky	Emerald Cricket
Jason Jink	Jungle Sky	Jason Jink
Soulslinger	Jungle Sky	Soulslinger
Dave Stewart	Subject:13	Dave Stewart/Ray Bleau
Boomish	Ism'assive/ISM	Boomish
Paradox	Stronghold	d.pandya/Strong 6
DJ Gunshot	No-U-Turn	Gunshot/Nico
Overcast	Bloody Fist	Overcast
Photek	Science/Metal Headz	Photek/R. Parkes
Dom & Roland		Dom Anges
Verbal Kint	Isatetrix	L. Jackson/S Miller/B. Bray
Square Pusher	Warp	Tom Jenkinson
Autechre	Warp	Autechre
Aphex Twin	Warp	Richard James
Capone	Hard Leaders	Capone
Pascal	Frontline/True Playaz	Pascal
DJ Hype	True Playaz/Ganja Kru	DJ Hype
Kosheen	Moksha	S. Evans/D. Beale/M. Morrison
Dirty South	M.A.D.A.B/Madbass	M. Kenney & B. Keith
London Elektricity	Hospital	Coleman/Goss
J. Majik	Defected	J. Majik
Mikey Finn		
Aphrodite		
Acetate	Flex	T. Francis
Narc 27	Narcotix	J. Greenaigh
Myer	Groar Attack/Carhartt	D. Myer
Talvin Singh	Omni/Island	Talvin Singh
Kenny Ken	Stricktly Business/Trueplayers	
Alec Empire	Grand Royal/Digital Hardcore	Alec Empire
Cybin	Emcee	Cybin
Ray Keith	Emcee	Ray Keith
UFO!	PNEUMA	UFO!
Ego Trippin'	Splash	Ego Trippin'
Elementz of Noize	Emotif	A Sides/Al Massive
Rantoul	Looking Good	Rantoul
Makato	L.G.R.	Makato

ARTIST	LABEL	ARTIST/PRODUCER
Pish Posh	Rawkus/Rawkuts	
John B.	Rawkus/Rawkuts	
Symbiosis	Tribe	Symbiosis
Bad Company	Virus	Bad Company
Search Engine	Reinforced	Search Engine
DJ Brockie	Undiluted	DJ Kane/Genotype
Instinct	Moving Shadow	G. Nicholls
A Sides	East Side	A Sides
Rayner	Formation	Rayner
DJ Red	Trouble on Vinyl	DJ Red
Ed Rush/Optical	Virus	Ed Rush/Optical/Fiere
Andy C.	Ram	J. Langston/D. Sparham
Adam F.	EMI	Adam F
UFO!	Sound Sphere	UFO!
Distorted Minds	Breakbeat Culture	J. Midwinter/A. Vickery
Maximum Style	Reinforced	M. Clair/D. McFarlane
Verbal Kint	Xsotetrix	L. Jackson/S. Miller/B. Bray
Gilberto	Ninja Tune	Cliff Gilberto

Webography*

The world wide web is a vast resource for you to gain knowledge on this topic. By typing keywords such as: jungle music, drum 'n' bass, or artist names into a search engine you can find infinite amounts of information.

WEB SITES
true-playaz.co.uk
recordings@moksha.demon.co.uk
madbass.com
hospitalrecords.com
warprecords.com
defected.co.uk
metalheadz.co.uk
jungleskymusic.com
theknowledge.com
ismrecords.com
omrecords.com
stageonemusic.co.uk
grooveattack.com
talvin.com
introactive.co.uk
kic.co.uk/undiluted
movingshadow.com
113audio.com/eastside
formationrecords.com
rawkus.com
home.att.net/~soundsphere/soundsphere@att.net
s7db.com
phunckatech.com
ramrecords.co.uk
theillfactor.com

ONLINE RECORD STORES
satelliterecords.com
breakbeatscience.com
Dancegrooves.com
611records.com
blackmarketrecords.com
groovetech.com
RewindRecords.com
compoundrecords.com
sales.grooveattack.com
virtualvinyl.com
grooveman.com
thedjstore.com
unclesams.com

*Compiled by Ben Bray, a.k.a. Benben—e-mail: Swaat13@hotmail.com